MAT

MW01119496

SIGNIFICANCE OF SIGNS

AUSTIN MACAULEY PUBLISHERS™

LONDON ★ CAMBRIDGE ★ NEW YORK ★ SHARJAH

Copyright © Matahari V. 2021

All rights reserved. No part of this publication may be reproduced, distributed, or transmitted in any form or by any means, including photocopying, recording, or other electronic or mechanical methods, without the prior written permission of the publisher, except in the case of brief quotations embodied in critical reviews and certain other non-commercial uses permitted by copyright law. For permission requests, write to the publisher.

Any person who commits any unauthorized act in relation to this publication may be liable to criminal prosecution and civil claims for damages.

The story, experiences, and words are the author's alone.

Ordering Information
Quantity sales: Special discounts are available on quantity purchases by corporations, associations, and others. For details, contact the publisher at the address below.

Publisher's Cataloging-in-Publication data
V., Matahari
Significance of Signs

ISBN 9781638293644 (Paperback)
ISBN 9781638293651 (ePub e-book)

Library of Congress Control Number: 2021920800

www.austinmacauley.com/us

First Published 2021
Austin Macauley Publishers LLC
40 Wall Street, 33rd Floor, Suite 3302
New York, NY 10005
USA

mail-usa@austinmacauley.com
+1 (646) 5125767

With loving gratitude to:

Philip Pinto for his presence on the journey,

Brian Beal for inspiring me with his transgenerational butterfly story,

Diya Thapar for introducing me to the 'Vision Quest' from her U. of T. class,

and the publishers, Austin Macauley, New York, for their work.

Table of Contents

Introduction

Who has seen tomorrow but the Signs?

This writing is a treatise on signs. The aim is to be aware, express feelings and not be ashamed of taking risks. It throws light on those unknown areas to make them known. Signs are the alpha and omega of things to come. Arising out of the unconscious, garbed in mystery, signs beckon us, warn us, and reveal much. We see them, we do not see them. Messengers and harbingers of things to come, they make us aware of the future. This opens up many a path we are to tread or where danger lies.

Signs vary in nature. They take the shape of phenomena, can be visual, auditory, and relate to senses. They can be intuition, coincidences, synchronicity, and dreams. One thing is common in all signs. They are loaded with subtleties and imbued with meaning. It is up to us to interpret them. It is here that culture plays a dominant role, as they are culturally constructed. The 'Swastika' is sacred in Hindu religion and anti-sematic in western religion. We cannot argue this. It is just different – not right – not wrong.

Conversational in nature, this writing points out how choices born of signs become chances for growth. Signs come from the unknown and the known. Unconscious and the subconscious. They are memories of past lives lived, future prophecies and more. It is this 'more' that I love to explore.

This is a journey into the unknown self- the subconscious. Where do we humans sit in the universe? Who calls us from the outer world? If we are connected to the unseen and the unknown where is this unseen and unknown?

Being an imagined reality, signs become observed and felt realities. Do we conceive them, or do they conceive us? Callings, predictions, and directions have a supernatural ring to them. We begin to feel them as a greater power guiding us. They are a part of religious and philosophical studies and translate into paranormal studies. Fascinating to explore, and challenging to comprehend, signs appear in our lives in many ways and at different times.

Signs of generosity, truth, and transparency shown by mother earth, were met with abuse. The perpetrators were We, the visitors on the planet. The wildfires of British Columbia, and Greece, earthquakes of Haiti, change of government in Afghanistan, and other peculiarities are Signs of nature wailing. Man may forgive, but nature does not. Hence, natural disasters and catastrophes. The law of karma comes into play, so does the need to watch for signs.

Digital age of data management looks at statistics and artificial intelligence as a sign of both progress and digress. Native intelligence, natural ability, face to face conversation, commitment, and loyalty to one another seem to be on a roller coaster ride. These are the signs of the times.

When I look back, I see that I was born thrice, and each birth was marked by a sign. When bells started chiming, they made me aware of this incarnation, of having a body, an opportunity to do good, a purpose to connect with humanity. This was my **first birth**. There was no fear, no anxiety, just curiosity and enthusiasm to get going with an explorer's spirit to the next portal. The spirit is the same today, the landscape has changed. I trusted my instincts.

My **second birth** was when being financially independent and fully aware, I walked into an arranged marriage, despite having options. The ring was a sign of responsibility in the role I had to play in the new life. The second birth today is also about getting rid of phobias and viruses of the mind that engulf one with fear. Signs of these are masks, vaccines, restrictions – all pointing to the language of fear and anxiety for a good reason of course.

My **third birth** was as a mother. The instinctual maternal in me emerged. It was a sign was one of temperance of my appetites and rendering myself so completely to the care of the family, that I forgot myself. Karma was at play. In each birth was a change, a growth, new learning, an emotional roller coaster ride!

Today ecological signs dominate us. We are called to protect the earth from global warming. The maternal in us, the Ying is revolting at man's greed. Aggression and chalice become a sign of the nurturing feminine. I was led once again to another portal of service and enlightenment. I learnt from my children and from teaching other peoples' children.

In later years, when my sister died of cancer at a young age, I did not take this as a sign of getting a check up done, till a biological sign appeared. I did not know that cancer is a silent killer. Then I went in for the knife and survived.

My time on earth became a sign to use my talents effectively. I began to write, something I had been putting off for years being involved in the nitty gritty, in the here and now situation.

Each tear became a responsibility to set right the wrongs, the ignored issues, the marginalized. I saw sublime feelings crushed under the weight of egos and persona, anxiety, and pressure. My heart bled when callous and crass people's decisions muted another. No one noticed butchered emotions, and silent treatment was met out to close files, as if people were objects to be trampled upon. In these dark corners I found light with the torch of Signs. Fumbling for solutions, I discovered meaning in life.

I write about building awareness, acknowledging, comprehending, and interpreting signs in daily life. Their broad trajectory covers the entire cosmos and speaks to all ages and cultures equivocally. They do not arise out of reason, so there is no point arguing them rationally. Results vary like perspectives. Their relevance and message is brought through an experiential lens, in life situations and more.

The **disguised Messiah** tries to connect. We do not recognize him and turn the spiritual into material. Caught in the nitty gritty of transactional living, we judge, disconnect, and decide parochially. Transformation comes through the transactional. WE learn through interaction with humans, nature, animals and signs. Attributes do not wear badges like goodness, loyalty, love, or fear. They spell themselves in interactions.

Body language is a sign of how we feel. Our emotions are an index of our state of mind. People frown, smile, make a face that expresses their emotion. This in turn is a sign of what is going on in their lives.

Fragile sensitivity rests in the soft **voice of our conscience**. Lost in the maze of inner and outer voices, we ignore the important for the urgent and comfortable. The voice of our conscience is not always pleasant. But it is always right. It is a reminder sign that speaks truthfully. Do we listen? We quieten it with our ego, busyness, partiality, conditioning and much more. It reminds us of the moral imperative of our decisions, actions, and words. Ego does not wish to hear it. Conditioning puts a lock on open minds. We face our mortality chained by our perceptions. Are we really free?

Signs become our **safety nets** and show us the way out. I realized this through travels and having a global family. I don't see how I would have survived without signs that helped. These came as strangers assisting me on the journey. They showed up just when I needed help. An example is Brian Beal who was on my journey all through the cancer detection and procedure. Br. Philip Pinto my mentor who at different points in time when I was down and out totally disappointed by another's silence helped me understand and deal with many a situation. These people became signs of existence for me.

The importance of signs cannot be overemphasized. We learn to earn in our youth, then in mid age we begin to manage the earnings, in later age to deploy it towards value-based giving; knowing we cannot take it with us. These are signs of passing through portals of being and becoming, growing, and evolving. Our attitude towards money, relationships, and life choices changes with growing years. What impressed us, attracted us diminishes and we begin to hear, see, and feel the signs.

Unless we escape the prison of the self, we cannot connect to the greater reality of love and embrace humanity. The dictum 'Turn left and you are left, turn right and you are right' examines these left and right turns in daily life. Welcome aboard to the transcendental flight of signs.

Genesis of Signs

"Relationships are measured not in time but in the learning, they provide."
– Brian Weiss

Let us explore the origin and effect of signs. **Signs come from the unconscious, the subconscious, and the conscious. They are a universal phenomenon arising out of an imagined reality, mythology, and history reflecting our beliefs, and our culture.**

They turn into weather reports, soothsayers, horoscopes, and have been our GPS in the past. Should technology fail us, they will become our GPS once more. Our sensitivity attunes to this reality. And we must not give the custody of our minds to the digital age which is rooted in primal signs. So is Artificial intelligence, based on native intelligence. Faith in our intuition, insights, and telepathy is our safety net. When everything changes, signs still remain our guides and like the northern star direct and illumine dark passages.

We are certainly living in exciting times of surreal alternative realities, questioning our sagacity. Bible is full of signs, so is the Holy Koran, the Hindu scriptures, and books of other religions. Surely there is a mystery about the sign language that escapes us. It has survived the knots of time. These can be prophetic, warning signs, road signs, signs of disease, signs of age, and more. It is this 'more' that I choose to look into in daily life, in interactions with ordinary people in life's circumstances. Weaved in their reality is the human condition and throwing light on it is the flashlight of signs.

This is what the signs do. They **relay messages**. In ancient times, pigeons were considered messengers and peacocks a sign of transformation. Heavenly minstrels like birds of all color are signs of transformation, resurrection, and transition. They showed up at my mother's widow sill when her time to depart arrived.

Every **emotion** holds a message. It is a **sign.** Feel it deeply. Honor it. Read it. Signs in science and mathematics are condensed forms of learning and memorizing. Each discipline is replete with its own signs. We heed mathematical signs and road signs to learn, and to be safe. Why not signs that help us discern and make wise choices? There are schools for literacy but none for universal wisdom of sign language.

By **sharing experiences**, we see how signs became condensed messages coming from a mysterious unknown through human interaction. I have asked myself if they are an answer to a need? Were they leading me to a place or a person? If so, what was the purpose? In all cases they made me think. It is through interactions that we learn. It is by communicating with nature that humanity finds connections. In this trajectory signs play an integral part by unifying, warning, and showing the way ahead. Another point of transition – a turn – another phase of a phase out, burn out, break out. Signs scream for attention and awareness. Preoccupied, we ignore them.

Prisons of fear can break with the gentle touch of unconditional love. Before the 'if only' becomes an excuse for not living and loving in full capacity, let us look at the signs emanating from within and without, and see what they have to say.

Having been guided by signs all along in my growing years, I began to trust them, discern their meaning and symbolic representation. They were succinct, had a language of their own, were not superficial and were always there. I saw their universality. A phone call at the right time, a page flipped, a bend in the road less travelled. I realized that sign language was comprehensible to all who chose to consider it. It fitted the specifics of time and age. Even children could see them, feel them, and make meaning of them. A child would suddenly smile at you and show his happiness. There was never a why to it. Happiness is a sign, just as crying was a sign that the baby wanted something. Learning to read signs is learning about human behavior, human need, condition, humanity en large. Emotions showcase themselves in body language and facial expressions.

There are **two views about guides** on the path. Some say they are 'the Supernatural' reaching us. Psychologists say they come out of aspects of our 'Unexplored self.' We have not yet owned nor integrated the unconscious source of signs in our personality. We question their sagacity.

Signs become an integral part of learning not only the three R's but '**help us discern before we decide**.' We can refer to them as a **lighthouse** as we sail through stormy waters. Feeling of calm is not an acquired art, it is a sign of well being, having good relations with everyone, being healthy and happy. Wildflowers, rivers and brooks, birds and bees hold answers by giving us signs of life, lessons in joy, another perspective to living. WE become signs and encounter synchronicities, intuition, serendipity, dreams, coincidences and more on the journey.

The frog in the well is content with the parochial boundaries of the well, till he jumps out of the well. **We discover our truth when we get out of the parochial prison of our perceptions, priorities, and perspective.** Then Humanity surfaces. We see it with another perspective, change our lens of perception, and our priorities change.

Signs reach us to a point in evolution and bring about **a paradigm shift**. We see the same things differently, imbuing them with understanding and meaning. Thereafter, it is up to us to take cognizance, to make choices. I invite the reader to explore the journey with signposts that guide and inform, yet leave the decisions to us.

How we use signs: Becoming aware of signs is becoming aware of two worlds: **Inner world** and **outer world**. In them rests the entire cosmos. **They can build an expectancy** and prevent a disaster by forewarning. Signs of sickness appear much before disease is diagnosed. The unconscious holds the secret to past lives. *Deja vu* experiences, meeting someone and having a feeling you have known them before, these and many other latent experiences surface as signs in our lives. They are compelling beliefs, thoughts and more. Yet, when you seek their roots, you do not find them in real life. Just in your conscious, subconscious and unconscious. No one knows how or when they originated.

Signs become **links to our past**, throwing light on who and what we were, are and connect us to the future. Our past does not leave us. In some chromosome, neural path it leaves tracks we have walked upon. Hence, the dread of heights, strong likes and dislikes confront us. WE are afraid for no reason at times and feel pleasant in the presence of some people and in some places. It is something inexplicable why we stop at certain junctures in life and feel history unfold. There are messages for us.

My father was sailing with the Royal British Navy, in the far east. One day, they arrived at an island in Southeast Asia. As he ventured into the thickets, he came across a life size statue of Shiva. Stupefied, he stood before it, thinking, *why in the world would it be in the middle of thickets and not preserved as a heritage?*

As he was thinking this when a voice said to him – 'you are going to face pain and danger, but do not fear, it will pass.' Perhaps this was a sign of something bad about to happen. He looked around. There was no one. Just this strong auditory sign. He returned to the ship. They had not gone far when my dad had an earache. It became worse as days went by, to the point of him losing his hearing. He thought about the sign, the statue, the warning, and the foreboding. Fortunately, penicillin was just discovered and available. It healed him. He realized the significance of the sign that had foretold him of the coming pain.

Signs **open a window of a reality that is more than the parochial view of the world.** The sensitive observe them, the non judgemental discern them. **Dreams** are the silent keyholes from which the human psyche emerges. They churn in the subterranean layers of the subconscious and emerge as dreams when the mind is rested and the body still. The outpouring emotion is a sign of what is going on in a person's mind, heart, and subconscious. Hypnosis takes effect through signs revealed by the patient.

They are **subtle harbingers of knowledge** that is not apparent. It is for us to discover, interpret and deploy them. They are physical, emotional, cultural, heritage and more. Often the mistakes we make in life are signs and turning points. Signs are explored by their interpretation in life experiences. A realization of a deeper truth. Each day we are bombarded by coincidences. Seldom do we ponder on these.

Carl Jung coined the word '**Synchronicity**' to combine the physical and the psychic. He stated that meaningful coincidences occurred outside the realm of cause and effect. Often when you think of someone, and the phone rings, it is a sign with a message for you to interpret. The word you were looking for, appears on a page. These are signs of synchronicity.

Through streams of consciousness, I explore deeper levels of the 'Unconscious' from which signs arise, whispering beliefs and messages from the future. Welcome aboard to the mysterious land of the unknown.

Our **interactions** with people in the universe bring people together. I received my answers from an experience I quote. I was flying from Delhi to Mumbai. The flight was full despite the fact that I had bought a ticket. I waited in the alley hoping to get a seat. It is as if the universe heard me. I saw the hostess approach. She showed me to seat in the business class. I suppose it was a VIP seat kept vacant till the last minute just in case someone showed up. Advancing to the seat I saw a Buddhist monk seated on the seat next to mine. He was looking out of the window of the plane. A thought struck me, *How do Buddhist monks travel business class?* It is as if he read my mind and turned around and gave me a big smile.

It was His Holiness 'The Dalai Lama'. I felt mesmerized by the warmth of his smile. He had caught on to my thought. I felt abashed knowing he had, smiled, and sat down beside him. Placing his hand on to mine as the plane took off, I could feel his grip tighten on my hand. He understood what I was going through in my mind. His holding the hand was a sign that everything was o.k. The journey lasted two and a half hours. If you were to ask me what did we talk about, my mind would draw a blank. His humor is so childlike one feels at ease immediately. He was answering my anxieties, and these were quite a few. A familiar chord was struck. Pristine affection from a total stranger who was much sought after something in me turned. It was perspective, paradigm or more? He spoke to me very simply but very relevantly of all that I was going through, and I felt embalmed by his words, answers to my unasked pertinent questions. These had been in my mind for years. Now, they were being answered. Was the overfull plane, the seat next to him, a sign that the Universe had answers for me? Gratitude had me listen intently. The experience and the vibrations of love and understanding have stayed with me ever since. It was more than a coincidence.

Once or twice, I tried extricating my had from his, but he held on. Powerful transmission of energy was taking place. My mind had travelled to a different zone. Time passed in a jiffy. When the captain announced the plane was landing, H.H.'s secretary seated on the back seat, asked me if I'd like a photograph of the Dalai Lama. Yes, I said and asked His Holiness to autograph it. "What should I write?" he enquired. "With love, to Mala," I replied.

He looked at me and smiled" You are naughty" he said laughing, I liked that adjective. It was the first time someone had used it for me. "Naughty?" I said. He was writing 'with love,' on the journey from Delhi to Mumbai in

English and in Tibetan. He handed me the picture and the surreal became real. I have it on my desk reminding me of Him. In His company I found myself. He noticed my insecurity without my saying a word. Meeting hm was a sign of transformation in a transactional world.

Every conversation has the potential for a larger meaning. It points out to something we can learn. But caught in our parochial perceptions, we begin judging people and planning our response. This exercise robs us of the essence of the message. The sign is lost.

Conscious listening is the only **route to deciphering signs.** Listening without judging, reacting, or blocking conversations, opens up a plethora of high energy fields from where signs come, and we can begin to comprehend better. **Deep listening** is needed in deciphering signs, determining paths, and having faith when things do not go right. We must choose the path. Signs are always there. All literature is found on sign language. It becomes an accumulation of fact and feeling we view from our lens – our perception. **Poetry is a systemized crunch of words, crackling insights with signs.** Religions breathe meaning into them. The deaf understand through sign language. The blind read braille.

We stand in the way of our evolution. Let us make **a list** of thoughts, words and deeds that have stalled our growth and well being. Were there signs showing us the way, signs we ignored or wrongly interpreted? WE will find there were alternate ways of handling situations that became worse by our lack of awareness and reactions. We needed to see the signs like stop, look and go.

Shifting our mind from what is before us, an illusional temporal reality to what is unknown and yet real like mortality, we split the two when they are connected. When aware of this truth we expand our wisdom box. Seeing correlations is step one to understanding the mathematics of life. When we move from illusory to the real, we find direction, gems and more.

Signs from loved ones: I had just entered the house after a short trip to India. The phone rang. It was my dad. "Can you return asap?' he said. There was an urgency in his voice that I had not heard before. A red flag went up. "Is everything fine?" "Are you well?" I asked. "No" was the response. It was not customary for hm to trouble anyone nor to speak about himself. I knew I had to go…

"I will," I said, and called my travel agent. The flight halted in Paris for an hour. We did not get off the plane. The seat beside me was empty. I felt a presence. My father was on the empty seat beside me. Was it my imagination? "You could not come to see me, so I have come to you." I knew it was his voice. The difference was that it was emanating from within me not from the outside as he had no body. This became a sign of his departure from this earth.

I later found out that was the exact time his spirit had left the body. The time I was in Paris. Hence, the Presence and the Voice. It added up. Paris was the one place he always wanted to send me, to study art. It never actualized. Now, we met in Paris. Ironically, I had Simone De Beauvoir's 'The Woman Destroyed' spoke to me in the plurality of the lives we live.

Sometimes there are different interpretations as signs do not come from reason but history and mythology. The snake is the most complex of signs. In Hinduism it is shown as a hood protecting Buddha, coiled as a seat for Vishnu, around the neck of Shiva. In Christianity it is temptation and the reason for eve and Adam to be cast out of the garden. Historically, the serpent represents creative life, a sign of rebirth and transformation. The serpent is a sign of higher consciousness in Hinduism. It is the voice of temptation in Genesis. The language of signs is the language of our **intuitive self,** the language of our unconscious. When we learn about other cultures our own becomes clearer. When we delve deep, we comprehend the meaning. Our ancestors deciphered time by looking at the moon and the stars. Newton discovered the law of gravity by watching an apple fall from a tree.

Phenomenology takes us to another level of perception. Here a person looks for meaning behind the phenomena. This search for meaning is the key to knowledge of the self and the other. The **Celts** feel that **mistletoe cures sterility** and is an **antidote to poison**. The Indian believe that ivory from an elephant tusk is an antidote to poison too. Emerald has curative properties. Unicorn has curative properties as used by the 4th century Greek Physician Ctesias. Sapphires and Jade are signs of true love along with red roses. Bare feet are signs of humility and the mendicants. In Indian temples, one must take off one's shoes before entering. People do that but seldom realize the meaning behind the ritual. Long hair are a sign of freedom and liberty worn by the warriors and by Hippies later.

Nature Signs: Fire is a sign with multiple meanings. It absolves the material, the sins, in Hindu religion. People worship fire in India. At birth and death and on all important occasions be they rites of passage like anointing a child or marriage fire is lit in 'mandaps' urns as a sign of sanctity. Trees are worshiped for their fruit, nurturing, wisdom, and teachings. Once my co teacher an Anglo-Indian downplayed nature worship calling it idolatry. I was offended. In our culture when you approach with sanctity, earnest will and good intentions you are building faith by pouring it in the object of your worship be it a tree a river like Ganges, the Sun or so. This was and is the belief of the indigenous in North America too. It is considered sacred in India. Its significance is its use during auspicious occasions like childbirth, child naming, marriage rituals and cremation. It has changed life ever since it was discovered. When we forget this nature reminds us with signs like the corona virus, floods, fires, and climates change. We still do not see these palpable signs. We squander the wealth handed down to us.

Elements of nature worshipped among indigenous tribes have significance as they revere nature by connecting with it. In this reverence is preservation of mankind. Signs of nature worship are not signs of idol worship, though they are interpreted this by many people who do not take the time to comprehend these. And we want to civilize them. I think we need to learn from them. We dehumanize when we disrespect human feelings. There is a connection between the Creator and his creation. The Giver and His gift. We take the gift, then question and blame the giver. The gift gains significance. The giver becomes insignificant. So, it is with the Creator and his Creation.

Marshall McLuhan's coined phrase, **'the medium is the message,'** is a universal truth. Signs are the medium and the message we need to comprehend. When put into social and cultural context, signs get imbued with meaning. This meaning is open to interpretation. Different cultures view it with their mythological lens, their folklore, traditional lens and more. **Hippocrates** the father of medicine identified bodily manifested signs to make clear states of physical and mental health. **John Locke** believed that signs enhance human understanding. In the semiotic theory, **Pierce** calls the signs 'effect on the mind by interpretation' a **'quasi mind** He sees signs through a philosophical lens. Just as knowledge cannot be reverted to ignorance, consciousness cannot be reverted. Once you have seen the truth of unconditional love, how can you go back to conditional and superficial emotion presented by crass commercialism, out of fear?

Signs are the **connecting principles**. Everything is connected to everything else. Spirits of man, animals, trees, oceans, stones and more. This universe has one creator, the vibrations of AUM sound and lightening are all signs of a world born, a world torn and reborn. In this cycle of creation and destruction signs play a role. What is this role and how can we best make use of it to prevent history from repeating itself, from falling prey to circumstance, traps that prevent liberation of the spirit. The answers are in the universe along with the questions. Why then are people not connected to one another? Are they blindfolding themselves? Are they listening to the ego?

Michael Talbot, like Jung, hypothesized that **internal experience manifests in the outer world.** Physicist Alain Aspect discovered that **sub-atomic particles can instantaneously communicate with each other, regardless of distance.** In doing so, concrete reality turns into psychoid reality. This is 'Synchronicity!'

Mystical happenings act as signs on life's journey. A butterfly flew into my living room, while I was finalizing the proof of a book dedicated to butterflies. It flew around my head for a few minutes, then flew out. A surreal experience! Then the moth, then again, the butterfly. My mind made a connection. Sometimes the unsaid says more than the said. So, it was with butterflies. By itself, a sign means little. Yet, in conjunction with society, religion, culture, medicine, business, art, literature, mathematics, and nature, it acquires a representational meaning. The meaning is contextual, fluid, and open to interpretation. It embraces the culture it comes from.

We can address '**Cultural Literacy'** as a 'language of different signs and phenomena.' There are multitudes of cultures that exist within me and are a part of my mental make up. Then there are multitudes of cultures outside me. These I embrace and they get assimilated into my culture. The trajectory gets wider, so does their meaning.

There are visible signs, auditory signs, tactile signs, olfactory signs, mystical signs, and dreams. "Follow your bliss," said Joseph Campbell. What is this bliss? What is mythology but symbols and signs, tales of heroes and villains, tales of courage to be oneself and more. Some people believe that 'some day a knight in shining armour will rescue them.' It does not happen that way. The medical men diagnose and prescribe accordingly. The educators use them. The parent uses them as markers. The heart looks for them. The importance of signs cannot be underestimated. Yet so few of us bother to look beyond our noses. We label them as 'superstition.' What we do not understand stymies us! The adventure lies in looking within, without, and in looking around. This builds awareness.

Nature Signs speak to us thunderously, raining down realities. We begin to decipher their language only when it is too late. Does this stop us from ravaging the earth, make us more human, listen to our spirit, animal spirits, and to harmonize with the cosmos? These questions need probing. Self serving become deaf to the calls of nature. Humanity gets buried, afraid of its insecurities peep afraid to leave habit. Stuck in cultural patterns, we fail to see that reality is but an illusion that changes with time. Yesterday is not today and today will not be tomorrow. Gifts of nature, time and energy are not to be thwarted. We make our comfort zones at the expense of mother earth, other creatures and fill our egos and belly with what we possess. Aren't we possessed by what we possess?

When we begin to operate from a place of comfort, a zone of narcissism, we miss **the signs.** We begin to wonder **why the viruses**, the plague, and other catastrophes occur. The geo-politics of the world, the tensions between superpowers like China and United States in 2020, is a sign of a worldwide calamity predicted by Nostradamus. Unless tensions de-escalate the fears that beset us, we will be **living on the edge or become the writing on the wall.** Which way we will go, depends upon the spiritual surgencies, intelligence and awareness. The earth is bellowing fire. The waters are cascading towards the land.

Where are the lifeboats, if not in signs?

We are not our thoughts. We are the **conveyer belts** transmitting thoughts. Therefore, relationship makers are greater than relationship breakers. They come from elsewhere for a larger humanity. They came to me that day from e mails from friends who cared. It made all the difference in seeing me through a difficult period of my life. And I am eternally grateful for the signs of affection and care. Divine works through human agencies for us. Peace is quintessential and the result of consistency and integrity. Signs can be prophetic, warning signs, road signs, signs of disease, signs of age, and more. Signs in science and mathematics are condensed forms of learning and memorizing. Each discipline is replete with its own signs. We heed to mathematical signs and road signs to learn, and to be safe. Why not signs that help us discern and make wise choices? There are schools for literacy but none for universal wisdom of sign language.

By sharing experiences, we see how signs became condensed messages coming from a mysterious unknown. I have asked myself if they are an answer to a need? Were they leading me to a place or a person? If so, what is the purpose of these synchronicities, dreams, attractions, coincidences we encounter in life? Can we learn from them and our ancestors?

I knew from experiences that they were not superstitions, nor imaginations but more. I realize one cannot rationalize signs, assess them, measure them nor judge them. They are not temporal nor transactional but eternal and of the Spirit. I invite you to join me on the journey. This is a journey of love and fear seen through the experiential lens of signs.

Interpreting Signs

"For as the lightning comes from the east and shines as far as the west, so will be the coming of the son of man."

– Mathew 24:27

Observe signs. They throw light upon life experience. Coming from the unknown, unventured and mystifying realms, they become voices, insights, and coincidences. Not knowing for who the bell will toll, anxiously we search for answers. They are all around us. Caught in our personal prison of fear we do not see signs of love till we lose it. Then the chase, the regrets. It is over. The road ahead reaches a dead end. We wonder.

Universal and timeless, the interpretation of Signs like Chinese whisper, is as varied as their language of applicability, identification, prophecy. Signs have survived the knots of time. They can be prophetic, warning signs, road signs, signs of disease, signs of age, and more. It is this more I seek to explore within the fabric of daily living and experiencing.

This writing arises curiosity and sensitivity and hopes to build an awareness of the signposts on the journey. **The disguised Messiah tries to connect**. We do not recognize him and turn the spiritual into material. Is this because he does not wear a name tag? Caught up in the nitty gritty of transactional living, we judge, disconnect, and decide parochially.

The transformational comes through the transactional. Attributes do not have names. WE assign them names like goodness, loyalty, love, or fear. These names become behavior signs. Discernment like diagnosis precedes perception and interpretation of signs, comprehending them or attributing them to cause or effect.

Body language is a sign of how we feel, how our emotions evolve and an index of what is to come. Fragile sensitivity rests in the soft voice of our conscience. Lost in the maze of inner and outer voices, we ignore the important for the urgent and comfortable.

The voice of **our conscience** is not always pleasant. But it is always right. WE quieten it with our ego, busyness, partiality, conditioning and much more. It reminds us of the moral imperative of our thoughts, actions, and words. Ego does not wish to hear it.

Conditioning puts a lock on open minds. We face our mortality chained by our perceptions. Our safety nets trap us. They build excessive fear. The only safety net is interconnectedness of humanity. Staying in and with love does not allow fear to stifle it.

Communication freezes when parochial limitations are set, and silos occur stating 'my way or the highway' mentality. I see a lot of destruction done by this, and the resulting ripple effects on people of all ages. Signs warn us, conscience speaks to us, but the ego is so insecure and overpowering that it feels it alone is 'Enough.' Unless we escape the prison of the self, we cannot connect to the greater reality of love and embrace humanity. This is their function. They release us from the narrow and open up the immense unexplored potential, moving hindsight into foresight and making the unknown, known. They relay messages.

In ancient times, **pigeons** were considered messengers and peacocks a sign of transformation. Heavenly minstrels like birds of all color are signs of transformation, resurrection, and transition. They showed up at my mother's widow sill when her time to depart arrived. Every emotion holds a message. It is a sign. Feel it deeply. Honor it. Read it.

'Turn left and you are left, turn right and you are right' examines these left and right turns in daily life.

Who has not looked up at the stars to see what they predicted when in a state of love or fear? Who has not played the game of 'she loves me, she loves me not?' Stuck in our perceptions, fear has immobilized us at times. This writing studies the silent language of signs in conversations, body language, dreams, coincidences, premonitions, intuition, synchronicity and more. It ponders upon their origin, their interpretation, usage, and cultural connections.

It questions our contribution to global warming. History repeats itself unless we are aware of where we stand and what we are doing or not doing in acknowledging it, learning from it to avoid catastrophes. Is the seen everything? Are there messages from the unseen world that are trying to reach us? If so, how do they reach us but by signs? I invite you to take the journey of planetary consciousness.

Tools to Interpreting Signs: When you see a sign use **intuition** to interpret it. Intuition takes you deep into your psyche or unconscious to explore its meaning. Many people are naturally intuitive. They are old souls who have journeyed far and long to come to a point of having insights. It is important to trust one's intuition. Each one sees the sign with a different lens. The following incidence proves the point. The birds of Lodi gardens in New Delhi, are famous for their variety and their colour. I sit watching them. Professor Ramchandra Gandhi is seated beside me in the lush lawn. We are conversing about his books *Svaraj* and *Muniya's Light.* The latter is about two Indian students returning from America after their studies in philosophy, light, and darkness. Their points of view. Professor Ramchandra Gandhi wants to turn it into a film. He asks me if I know someone.

"No, I don't," I say. We get talking about the other book *Svaraj*. This is close to his heart. It is a philosophical treatise. After a couple of meetings and attending his lectures, I am on my way back to Toronto. He wants to send some books to Canada. I decide to take a hundred copies and feel the market. I begin with Institutional sales. Libraries of various universities buy some. Collectors buy some. These are signed copies. A businessman buys the remaining lot for a foundation in United States. I am awed at the sales. *Why did this not happen in India?* I wonder. Happily, I wire the funds to the professor.

I do not know then that this was meant to be. Had I become a sign to assist the professor at this difficult time in his life. Struggling with his landlord in the April heat of India, Professor Ramchandra had no air conditioning in his rented apartment. The landlord was giving him trouble. There was clearly a disregard for his age and learning. I did not understand how a professor from Cambridge, a man of such learning and such a kind and gentle demeanour would have to go through such suffering. He was too independent to ask for assistance. Perhaps he trusted me implicitly; the trust being built by selling his books and helping with a grant for teaching a summer program.

The India International Center was his second home. It had a guest house. Upon receiving the funds, he moved into the India International Center. I received a letter of gratitude, with his manuscript of 'AUM.'

"It was work in progress," he said. Soon after receiving Ramu Ji's mail I had a dream. The Mahatma was sitting by my bed and saying something in his deep and sonorous voice. I could not decipher the words, but I recognized the voice from an audio tape I had heard of him in New-Delhi. I sensed gratitude. Then he was gone – the dream ended. I woke up.

Next morning, my son called me from New-Delhi to say that Professor Ramchandra Gandhi died at the I.I.C. guest house of heart failure.

"When did he go?" I asked my son. The time collided with the time in Canada, when I had the dream and a crystal-clear vision of Mahatma Gandhi sitting by my bedside, trying to tell me something.

Was this a sign of Ramu Ji's passing away?

What stays with me is the professor's loving kindness, of offering Diya his eye, to help Diya gain her sight in the one blinded by pressure on the optic nerve.

The next step to deciphering signs is to **watch the accompanying feeling**. Once you identify the emotion associated with the sign, please return to that point in life when had a similar feeling, had the intuition, and connected the dots. Memories will emerge. Uncover the message from these memories. The sign is often associated with the emotional state of a person. This combination of the sign and the emotion brings significance of that sign to surface.

Imagine you are the sign. Personify it. For example, say to yourself: 'I am the Lotus sign. I signify purity.' Say the first thing that comes to your mind. In it will be the revelation of how you feel truly. After defining signs in this way, watch how they interrelate. What is the message in the signs? Is it the same as before? Are the signs pointing you to recognize another, a transition, a truth, your authentic self, a need within you? Deep questions. You have been there before, you are called again, or warned or prophesized.

Making a **Sign Journal** on your personal journey is an interesting way of documenting signs as and when they appear. Dating them and illustrating them helps understand them. List the meanings against each sign. When it came to you, what your intuition told you about it, what was the emotion attached to it, what was your circumstance, were you in transition, how did the sign make a difference in your life? Put your assembled signs in a dictionary format. This is a self-awareness building exercise.

Having a mentor or **guide assists transitions**, life situations, choices and makes one aware of interpretations. Our journal becomes an invite to our guides. These can be spirits or real-life people. They come into our lives when we most need them. We may not know them by their names, positions, powers etc. but we often recognize them. How often have I heard from strangers: "I know you." as if memory had stirred some [past birth connexion.

In a quiet moment **reflect upon your guiding spirit**. Visualize the guide. Feel yourself surrounded by light and white protection. Give peace and blessings to it. After doing this ask your Guide for an interpretation of your sign. This can bring a lot of intuitive messages and insights. **Free association of thought** is another means of interpreting signs. Write down associated ideas, new, knew, few and see where your mind takes you. Be spontaneous, form patterns, decipher meanings. This may give you a clue to your insights, signs, dreams, coincidences and more.

Practice the game of **Pretence.** Imagine a body that knows nothing about your sign. Tell it bout your sign describing it in detail visually auditorily and other. The meaning of the sign becomes clear when you describe it.

Another way of interpreting signs is to look into your **Culture and Heritage**. Memory cells contain meanings of the signs. DNA is a strong unspoken unexpressed memory that harbours culturally relevant meanings of signs like swastika, water, birds, butterflies and more. Using a dictionary to find the meaning of the sign literally helps in discovering its added and implied interpretation, it gives you a starting point to research further.

Vision Quest

Vision Quest is a rite of passage followed by hunters from time immemorial. A tribal tradition for seeking signs. It is a long arduous journey taken by a young hunter during his rite of passage deep into the forest alone. The purpose is to receive greater understanding of nature, Spirit power, knowledge of animals, their ways, build resilience and fortitude and a survival strategy. He depends entirely upon signs. Followed by the indigenous people of North America and Northern India this rite is reflective of the connection between the spirit of animals, nature, and man. It binds the cosmos together.'

Alone and hungry he must survive the thickets, make his shelter, get to know himself and attune himself to the Spirit world. This is his education, his survival kit. Deep green forests become his classroom. He drinks from the brooks and streams and hunts for survival. There is danger of wild animals devouring him, him being lost. He prays to the animal spirits to guide him, to forgive him and gets to know them before hunting. This is his homework. Fearful and passionate about exploring, he sets afoot in the unknown, to experience for himself that which will make him a good hunter. On the way he meets many ordeals. Undefeated, he prods on. He falls prey to his mistakes and is guided by spirits he connected with. Seeking forgiveness, before hunting makes the kill a sacred sacrifice. With the help of a mentor, he prepares for this journey. It starts with creating a medicine wheel, a circle made by placing his favorite stones circular on the ground in preparation for the vision quest, a sacred place for contemplation. The medicine wheel represents seasons, life, and rebirth and is a sign of healing just as Raphael is the recognized saint and a symbol of healing.

Almuth was a young traditional German girl who stayed with me for three months during her *'rite of passage.'* She was dressed in her traditional attire when I went to collect her from Mona's place. Mona was an assistant professor of Anthropology at University of Toronto and a friend. I had a large house.

Mona suggested I take in Almuth Gutner, nee Ali. It was a wonderful experience. Dressed in black with a guitar in hand, black boots and a black wide hat, Ali looked every bit a traditional German. I was curious to know more, as she entered my car. We drove in silence. Upon reaching the house, Ali shared a room with my daughter Diya. We had long conversations about Germany, the passage of rites in different communities. Ali was paying her way through North America. She came with no money, did not accept any, earning her way by playing the guitar. She found hosts, was giving of her soulful gift of music helping wherever possible. Towards the end of her journey, she wanted me to drop her to a truck station where she could hitch a ride to Vancouver.

I respected her wish and dropped her at the closest gas station. A month later I got a card of gratitude from her, from Hamburg, where her parents lived. Both were high school teachers. Ali was completing her degree in Berlin. Only thrice, she had called her parents, once each month – that is all she was allowed by her rules. In two weeks, she had helped put the disorderly basement in place, organized everything and labelled it. Could I have asked for more? I congratulated her parents. My admiration for the organization skills of the Germans was confirmed. For me, Ali had become a goodwill ambassador of Germany. Ali became a sign of human will power and goodness. "One can achieve whatever one sets one's mind to." Ali travelled North America following the signs that pointed her direction and were a part of the rite of passage.

Sense and Sensitivity

We learn from animals before we begin to train them. We learn about love and fear. They teach us by their sensitivity and sign language. Which trainer of horses has not been kicked? By this he learns about the nature of the horse, his likes, and dislikes, and what irks him. He becomes sensitive to his stead. In this interaction is love. That which begins as fear ends in trust.

Horses are sensitive and loyal animals. It is a sensuous feeling to ride. The feeling of being one with the horse's trot, to gallop as 'one' body and 'one' soul, is a love relationship! Both understand each other's body language. They commune as they stride, with their moods on the same wavelength. We can learn from them. They heal. Yet some are afraid of the unknown responses of the animals. When we approach them with love they respond favorably, as is seen in many stories both real and mythological. The horse is afraid of the stranger. Then the love sign, the sensitivity shown by the would-be rider by patting him, opens communication. It is a form of courtship. An ice breaker. A loving personality is not a stranger to anyone. Love is not a persona, a personality alone, but an attribute imbued in character. It is in understanding the emotion, its giving and receiving nature that we feel affection.

The relationship between a rider and his stead is gratifying. His eyes beckon you. He senses how your body moves with his, in perfect alignment.

Here is a true story of signifying a horse's intelligence. Sri Ganga Ram was a forest officer, in northern India. Attuned to nature signs and animal spirits, he spent his entire life in the deep and dark forests, riding horses, engineering the construction of dams like the Bhakra Nangal dam, and swimming in rivers. He was passionately fond of Sultan, his favourite horse, and spent time with animals, flora, and fauna. He lived in the lap of nature as a part of it.

One evening, returning home from a dinner party, he had barely gone a few yards when Sultan stopped. It was pouring heavily. *That was not the reason for Sultan to stop.* Ganga Ram wondered. Transfixed he waited in the rain for a while. Then he turned around and made his way home by another route through the forest. Next morning, he rode to the same place where Sultan had paused. He saw a large ditch filled with rain water. There were snakes around. Sultan had sensed this, and Ganga Ram had trusted Sultan. He patted his steed and got down.

Ganga Ram felt something crawl up his breeches. It was a cobra. Having encountered them before, but not at such close quarters, Ganga Ram held his breath. He did not panic nor move. He told me later, that was the way not to 'threaten' the animals and reptiles. When threatened, animals react. I learnt that truth from my grandfather. It applies to humans too. The cobra climbed down his breeches and went his way. Ganga Ram breathed again, knowing he had respected the cobra, Sultan, and himself. In doing so, he had stayed safe. I was amazed, that he knew the language of the animals so well. It was his survival strategy.

Jesus knew his power over nature when he performed the seven miracles. They reinforced faith. Choices and chances work together, like the horse and the rider. Both need to have faith in each other and to align with one another. It is a soulful relationship; in it both feel free and emancipated. Test is a sign of faith not just knowledge. "Have a good alignment strategy make wise choices," he would say.

Alas! I thought years later, *each generation must discover for itself that the stove is hot.* We must blunder to pay heed to the warning signs of thunder and go through the throes to understand the lessons learnt.

The Chalice and the Blade

Gender distinctions are not inequities but signs of what each gender was made for.

We may transcend limitations, but there are somethings we cannot change.

The chalice is a sign of the feminine qualities of tenderness and gentleness, nurturing and nourishing. The blade stands for male aggression and violence. These signs typify the two genders. They signify different roles. Today technology is decrying the roles and reversing them. Signs stand questioned. Yet, their significance cannot be underestimated.

Reine Eisler, in her book, *The Chalice and the Blade,* asserts the cultural perspective of the signs. She places areas where the women dominate the work field and the males the household. Though the world has changed a hundred and eighty degrees, some Indigenous tribes still follow this. This demarcation did not mean that women had less of cognitive power. There are no measures in signs and Truth. Only in accounting for behaviors. It is seen that the first mathematician who discovered the zero was a woman and it was found inscribed as a dot on a temple in Gwalior, India. There are several stories that speak of this amazing mathematical discovery.

Romance is a sign of two people in love. Children are brought into the world and nurtured not by test tubes but loving care. This love is a sign of the feminine. God is referred to as a She, a nurturing feminine. There seems to be a change. The angry 'He' God was feared in the past. In a gender driven world. God became a gender. Fear ruled then. With gender equity love is taking over now. Yet, there is a potpourri of confusion as signs and their denotations sit in the center. They vary in the global world. The answer is partnerships, seeing together, complementing and complimenting, caring, and daring to express one's authentic self.

In patriarchal societies women were objectified, perceived in the role of a mother, sister, lover, wife and got trapped by the role. Their voice took a long time to be acknowledged, appreciated, and honored. There was hierarchy in the system that built barriers in communication.

One such story illustrates the victimization of women during war. Upon the partition of India in 1947, I the disputed part of Kashmir, several women were captured, raped, and returned as prisoners of war. When they returned after peace was established, their husbands would not take them back, they were ostracized. Socially unaccepted, they resorted to suicide. Tattoos wore signs of clans, cultures, and identification marks. They were certainly not fashion symbols like tattoos of today. The tattoos on the returned women prisoners' bodies had bracketed them as 'impure.' These signs screamed societal changes. Humanity had taken a back seat. The madness of hegemony and war took precedence over everything else. Where was culture, tradition, respect and the sacred in all this?

One morning in the village of 'Akhnoor,' in the undivided Kashmir – conflict broke out at the border. The cook was boiling milk in a large copper vessel on the stove. A bullet came and went right through the pot. He startled and ran to inform the occupants. Soon there came cries of people, sounds of fury were everywhere. People were running around in a tizzy. There was a blaze. Signs of destruction! Karam Chand had four daughters, the youngest was just born. He got everyone to go to the basement. Then he set a fire at the entrance of the house as a protection sign. Seeing the fire, soldiers went past the house, thinking it was already targeted.

His family was saved. The youngest child began to cry. To keep her from attracting attention, Karam Chand scuffled his baby. His wife was beside herself with anguish. But she knew if he had not done so, the soldiers would have captured the other girls and victimized them. Under the cover of the night, everyone who could, did escape Akhnoor with the kafila.[1] Women and children, old and young all piled up on donkeys with bags of essentials – dogs and hens – in the cover of the night and left for Srinagar. Ma's baby sister was turning blue. Her situation medically signalled 'critical!' When the caravan stopped by a stream, so women and children could quench their thirst, Karam

---

[1] caravan

Chand got down his horse and put a few drops of water in the baby's mouth. It trickled down. Upon reaching Srinagar, he took her straight to a hospital. Here she was treated, and life restored. It was a miracle – a sign of who controls the imparting and ending of existence on earth. Life came alive! She is a professor emeritus of History, in Kanpur, India today.

So, it is with love. It makes us go beyond ourself and look for meaning in another. It is not a self fulfilling but another fulfilling prophecy. Life is lived at all portals fully. Love is not a fancy, a like or a dislike.

Fear and Love

"There are no coincidences in love."

– Brian L. Weiss M.D.

Who has not looked up at the stars and wondered about love, afraid of losing them and felt fear? How can you love someone when you possess them, or are possessed by them? That is not love. **The alphabet 'L' stands for love. It also stands for liberation**.

Love is liberation from the parochial perspective. It is not an encaged bird. Birds like to fly, to sing their songs free and clear. No one judges their song nor measures it. Beyond the strands of limitations, they have a mystery, so does love. IT is mysterious and reached us in multiple ways through our unconscious, the breath that created us, the blood that flows through our veins and the nerves that make sense of it all. Love is the essence of us as we are. This is the sign of love – to be accepted and to accept. You cannot reject truth and if love is truth, it will never be rejected. It is a gift of the soul from one to another.

People who associate love with jealousy, to have and to hold are seriously fooling themselves. Love can't be held. It can be given, nurtured, set free but seldom understood, reasoned or handled logistically. It is a sign of Spontaneity and Grace. It does not wither with age.

Love was in the beginning of creation and will be in the end. The **illusory drama** of human existence on earth continues in between. Written in a reflective and conversational tone the writing brings home this truth by unveiling synchronicities, coincidences, dreams, chemistry in human behaviour and unifying the world of birds and bees, butterflies, and horses. The tone is conversational, observational, and reflective. The **trajectory and the test are the human condition** in a diverse cosmos of flora and fauna in which we humans dance to the tune of the stars or cringe under the pressure of circumstance. **What matter is not what is done to us but how we receive it with gratitude or attitude, and by so doing how we treat another.**

The mystery comes through with Krishna's 'Raslila'[2] set into motion by vibrations. These help us evolve and calibrate energy at higher or lower levels depending upon the path we choose. There are always signs on the way. It is how we read them, interpret them, comprehend, and apply them so no regret situations are maintained, and history does not repeat itself.

People don't die of the disease; they die of the fear of it. It destroys them before it really kills them. Similarly, people do not fall in love but rise in love to higher energies and inspiration by affirmation and validation. We can see their signs in good health or ill health, joy or depression, productivity and proactivity and the attitude of 'just getting by. Fear and love are two great motivators in life. They have altered the course of history and signs of these are evident in architectures like '**The Taj Mahal,**' kingdoms won, and kingdoms lost, wars and more. They have turned the course of economics, society, and politics at the same time imperceptibly. We see their effects but seldom examine the causes. This is because the signs rest in the foundational emotions and not in the results emanating from these. Shah Jahan the Mughal emperor built the Taj Mahal for his beloved wife Mumtaz Mahal. He never though he was building a memorial to outlast him and be an icon of true love. He never thought he would be imprisoned by his son and would see the Taj from behind the bars. Both love and fear were at play. When we love, we give the best of ourselves. When we fear or others fear our power, they imprison us in slots of their minds and silence, in cubicles where one lives just to breathe. This is what happened. The Taj is a sign of both love and fear.

Love is an active force that looks for the interest of another and is not self serving. Thomas Merton puts it beautifully in these words: "Love is our true destiny. We do not find the meaning of life by ourselves alone – we find it with another. We do not discover the secret of our lives merely by study and calculation in our own isolated meditations. The meaning of love and living in our life is a secret that must be revealed to us in love, by the one we love."

_____

[2] World of illusion

Listening to my parents was an act of love even when I did not always agree with them. Understanding the demands of my husband's career as a fighter pilot kept me from stressing him for anything. I always had this fear and signs of pilots crashing during sorties. Pilot error be it stress, birds or wrong decision did it. I did not want this to happen to him. It taught me patience.

Love can translate into gratitude, faith, consideration, empathy, and fear of losing the loved one. There is a difference in being in love and loving. Love practised is loving actively, and love fantasized is being in love.

Love does not subject itself to power and control, being measured or measuring. It is the **language of the heart** not taught in any school with a curriculum. In its folds lie secrets of mortality and immortality. It is beyond right and wrong, beyond judgement, classification, or negativity.

Listening is loving. Seeing is loving. Believing is loving. Signs have proved the presence of love and fear many a time and when followed the signs have led to overcoming adverse circumstance. This proves that nothing is cast in stone and man by his will and good intentions can alter the course of history. People have connected across oceans without technology but with love and telepathy and kept relationships going.

To venture fearlessly and to love with every fibre of one's being is to enter the garden once more. Co travellers are likeminded soulmates, kindred spirits we can turn to for guidance. They may have passed on to another realm, but they are there in the ether, in their words, memories, tasks they undertook and completed. Their example becomes a sign of things shaping up if we follow a certain path. growth, they are our mirrors and we theirs. Creating a curated space for spiritual partners on this journey helps me make a quiet and uninterrupted connection with my spirit

"Think about it this way; when something occurs beyond chance, to lead us forward in our lives, we become more actualized people. We feel as though we are attaining, what destiny is leading us to become. When this occurs, the level of energy that brought about the coincidences in the first place, is instituted in us. We can be knocked out of it, and lose energy when we are afraid, but this level serves as a new outer limit which can be regained quite easily. We have become a new person."

– Father Sanchez

All relationships are shaped either by love or by fear. Our actions and reactions arise out of these. Both emotions are masked. Both are fundamental to life. Upon them decisions are based. Our happiness and success emanate from these. In them lies our ability to evolve. They affect our liberation, and our well being. Why then are we afraid to express unconditional love? Why do we not acknowledge and deal with fear, instead of partnering it? The reason to my mind is in patterns, perceptions, priorities, and conditioning.

Love is a sense of belonging, there is a palpable connection. People outgrow their families but not the love of the land they are connected to. It calls you in different ways. R.K. battled with this. He was an architect of Indian origin who had spent his entire life studying architecture in Tokyo and practising it in New Delhi. In his twilight years he wanted to settle down in the place of his ancestors. Looking for signs he finally found one. He was in Udaipur, Rajasthan – the state of his birth and ancestors. It was a windy day. His turban flew off and landed on the steps of Udaipur Lake. R.K. ran after it. The tranquility of the lake spoke to him. It was his sign of having arrived at his destination. Udaipur became his place of retirement. It was the place of his ancestors. Here he lived till the end.

Signs of love are as numerous as the stars in the sky. They have a common denominator. The lovers recognize them. The unheard is heard. Similarly, fear is a powerful motivator and expresses itself in sign language. Our physical bodies respond to it, cognition gets impaired and self protection becomes the key motivator.

Active Love: Love in my parents' marriage was present decades after they married. Mum was a vegetarian. Yet, she took lessons in non-vegetarian cooking as my father enjoyed mutton curry and loved to shake the marrow off the bones. This was perceived as sign of her love for him, in days when people did not openly say 'I love you' to one another. He in turn never missed getting her jasmine flowers she so loved. These she twirled around her braids. I saw them as signs of 'love' that became rituals and sacred signs like fasting on Friday for her husband's health and on Tuesday fasting for her children's welfare. These signs reassured relationships as reminders of active love. If they were angry with each other, we never noticed it, as signs of love were always present to make up.

Shakespeare says in one of his sonnets: *'Let me not to the marriage of true minds admit impediments, love is not love that alters when it, alteration finds. Love is not love that alters when it alteration finds.'*

The respect in their relationship was surreal. I realize this is not the case in contemporary society and this was predicted in the Bhagavat Gita When marriages fail, children will get affected adversely as is seen. The question is:

Is it worth the while to expose the children to a bad situation in a bad marriage? Some situations have no chemistry? Can we create this chemistry?

Answers will vary according to experience. Love is not necessarily staying together in body. It can be and is a responsibility that can be shown even when apart or with one who has chemistry with is. There is no complete ditto, no customization of our expectations. What every one seeks is to find a place to grow, be nourished and nurtured to eb their best self going forward. This is universal. world of walk in love, walk out indifference attitude. It is not that there were no signs of temptations, weaknesses, points of difference. But that truth of their bond and chemistry overcame it all. They found joy in relating, communicating and being together. Not always but most of the times. This made a difference and in turn to how we grew and related to the world around us, it built our values and our vision. While they are gone, their example stays. Trusting comes naturally. Fear strangles trust for those who have grown with an if or but strategy.

I saw signs of partnership when he made her the first cup of morning tea, and she would make the second. I never saw her nag or doubt him regardless of how many beautiful women surrounded him or of the call of his duty. I am sure they had their bouts of anger. But rarely if at all, did I see these. Perhaps because they communicated intimately, clearly keeping love alive. An 'agree to disagree' policy dominated their relationship. Signs like him getting her flowers for her long hair upon returning from work and she cooking him his favourite dishes, strengthened the bond. **Romance was never lost**. The twinkle in the eye was as sign of it. It stayed long after he was gone, along with the warm texture of his voice.

I grew up in the ambience of passion, excitement, understanding, trust, and acceptance. Role modelled, they got imbibed in me. This was education to me and their gifts. They became my strength and helped build resilience in later years.

Mum was lost without him. It appeared as if she waited to join him eternally. Her face would light up at the mention of his name. He was still there for her. He is still here for me. *Is his spirit reincarnated in Paris?* I wonder. That is where I found his consciousness reach me. It follows not the path of 'ignorance' but that of 'enlightenment,' is said of the Spirit. You do not fall in love; you rise in love with clairvoyance of the Spirit.

When you think of somebody, sometimes they are thinking of you too. It is a sign that you need to contact them. When there were no telephones, telepathy worked, and thoughts became messengers and receivers. The cords were vibrations, signs arising from the sixth sense.

The more you follow your intuition the more in sync will you be with the universe. Many times, it is about clearing the negative energy to create pathways to positivity. The universe responds to our inner yearnings mysteriously by bringing people into our lives to answer our questions, befriend us, save us from catastrophes, be a shoulder to cry on.

For mum love was not about expectation nor perfection. She did not believe in perfection. She believed in being humane. It was the very purpose of her existence.

In this jaded world of sorts, when we take the other for granted, we put love on the back burner without understanding or activating it as a force of change, resilience, progress, and results. Seldom do we see its value and potential in shaping our lives. It becomes transactional not transformative. We shy away from the acceptance of this awakening and recoil in self consciousness, tuning our perceptions to the hum drum norm.

Before love can blossom, it gets tarnished by perceptions. People see love according to what the media projects. Seldom do they see it as a cure for society's ills, a belief, and a need for getting through the passage of time with tenacity. We need to escalate and excavate this sublime commitment of 'love,' so bestowed upon us as an invaluable gift, a value and make it apparent to a world blinded by selfishness. The pandemic of the 2020 is a sign reminding us that we cannot take people, health, time, and life for granted.

The following experience explains how signs of love and fear impact people.

Each Thursday, I ran a book club at my place in the Air Force base in Ambala. Ladies came in, we read from books, caught up with the happenings and departed. One such Saturday, I was laying out the table for tea, getting the books ready for reading when Donna walked in with her newly born son 'Jonathan.' Donna was a medical doctor. She knew what to expect post childbirth and all new mothers trusted her. She knew the staff of the Army hospital. This was an asset. Her husband Benjamin was a fighter pilot too. Donna asked me for some money to pay the rickshaw man, as she had forgotten her purse. This I did. She asked if she could use the bathroom. "Of course," I said.

Soon after the readings and the refreshments ladies dispersed. Donna was the first to step out with baby Jonathan. Within minutes, one of my friends came in running, panicking: "Donna was lying unconscious on the road." Jonathan had fallen from her hands, into a dry gutter outside the boundary wall. Fortunately, he fell on the leaves that had just been raked and stored there. Together we went out to retrieve Jonathan and Donna. When I went to the bathroom to wet a face towel, so she could regain consciousness, I was surprised to see empty vials of morphine in the sink, and an injection on the side table. A red flag went up. I rushed to call the squadron. The person at the other end said Benjamin had just landed from a sortie, if could I call later. I said I would wait. It was urgent.

Benjamin must have sensed what happened. He did not change from his flying suit but rushed and began searching her handbag upon arrival. In the bathroom used by Donna, there were empty phials of morphine, and used injections. Benji knew then, she had overdosed. She was a medical doctor suffering from an addiction and had an easy access to morphine at the hospital. This is what Benjamin feared. I was aghast! For the first time I was seeing someone so educated, a friend, in a helpless situation. Picking up Jonathan and then Donna, he rushed to the staff car and drove off in some frenzy. The memory of this experience encapsulates both his love and fear. I could only imagine his daily battles with both these elements.

He told me later, that he was aware of Donna's addiction but his love for her was greater than his fear and he took upon himself to help her rid herself of this nasty addiction. Now there was Jonathan too.

Years later, I met Benjamin and Donna at another Air Force base, where we were posted. The first thing I did, was to go and see how they were doing.

Benjamin had been a chain smoker when I knew him last. He had given up smoking completely. Donna had given up drugs. Jonathan was growing well. His sacrifice was a sign of love that sustained the relationship and three people. Love had triumphed. There was mutuality, reform, harmony, and peace. Staying the course with the spirit of faith was a sign of their love for each other. What if neither had co operated or one of them had tried and failed? Signs could alter destiny only with patience, belief and will from both, if there is chemistry and recognition.

Our best music and art are reflective of us confronting our fears. It is so close to the bone; it breaks us before it makes us more resilient.

"Red, Green Orange – I love these big dots – what are they?" asked the child.

"Road signs," said his mother.

"Why are they there?" Then abruptly, "When you fell in love with Dad, were there signs to tell you to stop, look and go?" His curiosity was awakened. She was amused at his questions and continued the conversation. The child learnt to pause at stop signs, look and proceed accordingly. As awareness grew, he became conscious of other signs, in mathematics, chemistry, religion, medicine, and more. These were simple and complex signs. When he peeled the onion of semiotics he was mystified by the many interpretations.

He read about Mark Twain's dream: Meteors were seen when Mark Twain was born and when he died. 'Mark Twain dreamt that his brother had been killed and lay in a metal coffin, a bouquet of white flowers was on his chest with a red blossom in the center.' Although his brother on that date was still alive and well, it was only a month later that Mark witnessed the scene of his prophetic dream. 'His brother was killed in a boiler explosion on a Mississippi steamboat. When Mark went to see him, he saw the metal coffin, the white flowers, and the red blossom.'[3]

The young man now began to read the signs differently, adding another dimension to them – one of prophecy! He realized the two bookmarks. The beginning and the end encapsulating all the in between had signs of birth, signs of life, signs of death. All consciousness emanated with Signs. Our first cry telling the parents of our physical needs and all along on the journey through

---

[3] Guy Murchie in The Seven Mysteries of Life

this world, there were signs emanating from the unknown and the known speaking to us. Did we stop and listen or simply turned away much to our loss and anguish?

To be in love with the universe, is to relate to it in multiple ways. Signs, symbols, intuition, synchronicity, and serendipity become lenses for viewing and comprehending life and its course.

Transgenerational Love

"The important thing is not to think much but to love much.
And so, do that which best stirs your love."

– St. Theresa of Avile

"I would have given these two monarch butterflies to my grandmother when I was probably about five or six years old – that would have been around 1965. Grandma Beal passed away in 1996 – and this match box was found with the two butterflies in it when the contents of the house were being gone through. Remarkably, instead of being tossed into the garbage, they were recognized as a gift from me – perhaps Grandma had told my dad about these butterflies. They came back to me. They have rested quietly in the same box into which they were lovingly placed more than a half century ago. This is a story of love transcending generations."

– Brian Beal

What makes it more dynamic, is the fact that these 'moving flowers' as the poet Robert Frost calls them, sensed the love of a six-year-old Brian. Touched by the recognition of their beauty. They made an easy joyous catch. Brian brought these lovely monarch butterflies to Grandma Beal, as an offering of love.

Both Brian and his grandma became conveyors of love and transcendence of the temporal. The story of the butterflies has several layers to it and unfolds thus. In 1996, when Grandma Beal dies, and the house is cleaned, the monarchs are not thrown away. Brian's father returns them to his son. This is second generation love.

From 1996 till present time Brian keeps them safely in his sock drawer. The interesting part is that the butterflies do not dismember. Untouched by time, they look as fresh as when Brian had just caught them. This is third generation love. A continuing thread connects across the generations through space and time.

The fourth dimension is expressed by the silent but powerful language of the butterflies themselves. Their soulful longing for love waits patiently for the moment they will be united with their counterpart monarch butterflies from across the ocean. This happened without anyone knowing or being conscious of it. Time and space are transcended by eternal love. Humans become agencies of transporting this longing. This is how the east and the west met through the silent language of the butterflies. Two monarch butterflies preserved on a plaque as an art form, were presented to me by the Eastern Air Command after I delivered a lecture on 'Paradigm Shift' in 1996. Incidentally, this is the same year that Brian was presented with the butterfly plaque by his father after his grandma died. I brought them with me out of all the things I left behind. I was told that butterflies were a sign of transition, change, hope and joy. They were my companions in my move from India to Canada. Often, I would meditate on the two monarch butterflies in many a vacant hour and think of transition and change. This would give me the hope and strength to persevere in my endeavors as a mother, as a writer and a teacher. The butterflies seemed real and had a presence.

One afternoon, two decades later, as I was contemplating on the plaque, I noticed it tilting to one side. I got up to straighten it and it fell into my hands. The thought of the butterflies falling into my hands symbolized a message – a transition, a transformation.

I thought of Brian transitioning from his long-held job. It was a period of change, hope, courage, fortitude, and creativity. Everything the butterflies signified. A thought crossed my mind. *Why don't I give the butterflies to him?*

I acted on it, little knowing about the two monarchs he had caught at the age of six. And they lay in his sock drawer waiting for their eastern counterparts. I read the language of patience of the butterflies meeting each other. It was poignant and made meaning.

The thank you note from Brian carried a picture of two monarch butterflies in a matchbox with their story. Monarchs caught and held in the spirit of love in North America were placed in the plaque with butterflies from Shillong in India. I do not know why pout of all the honorariums, I brought the butterfly plaque to Canada. Something had caught my inner eye. I grabbed it and with my few possessions. Perhaps it was to give it to Brian in 2020. He had the other two monarchs from 1996. His catch at an early age of six, perhaps three decades before 1996. This may sound synchronistic, yet it has a timeline and holds a sign of interconnectedness. If this is not a story of the timelessness, of transcendental love, faith, and hope, what is it?

Transcontinental Signs

"We possess many ways of sensing one another at a distance."
– George Leonard, 'The Ultimate Athlete.'

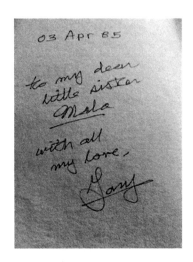

The envelope read: Gary E. Moore, 800, 10th St., East Bethany, New York.

Inside it was "THE BOOK' by Alan Watts, with the note below. This was the last of the many gifts, I received from a brother I had never seen or met.

Gary is no more, but his address has stayed with me. It is an incredible story of synchronistic growth – of two spirits who intertwined but never physically met in material form. Yet, they communicated regularly and familiarized each other with the trajectory of their being. This is also an Indo-American story of two cultures, woven over two decades with sensitivity and loving care. For those who do not believe in platonic relationships, here is an example of one.

We spend our lives chasing fancy images – struggling with guilt or missed opportunities. Soon the curtain is down! The show is over. While the world applauses we are not there to hear the sounds. The moment is lost forever. Nothing can recall the past hour. It turns to memory as my pen friend Gary has. With this memory we communicate. We sift it, in our endeavour to see what could have been done differently.

In my growing years, it was common to have pen pals.

I made a pen pal in United States – Gary E. Moore. He was studying architecture in Boston, and I was completing my Senior Cambridge.

His fondness for Mahatma Gandhi and his appetite for Indian culture, literature and poetry brought us together. He called me his 'little sister' across the seas. Each week, usually on a Thursday, I received a letter from him, sometimes a parcel of books, clothes, cards, and envelopes with sachets of tea and lavender. I got a rosy picture of what Americans were like in the seventies and eighties.

Thursdays became special to me. I had received Gary's address from the pen pal section of "Teenager" a magazine I wrote a byline for. After finishing school, I went to a Teachers' College – Gary went on to designing buildings and houses. Very introspective, he studied the needs and characters of people who were going to live there. Often, he reminded me of the character of Howard Roark from Ayn Rand's book, *The Fountainhead.*

Gary was consistent with his weekly letters. They kept me updated about what was going on in the U.S. – and his love for gardening and cultivating mini oranges and herbal teas on his farm. At that point in time when there was no e-mail, the postman was eagerly awaited. We were two people from different cultures and different backgrounds, who had come together as kindred souls.

I finished university, and got a teaching assignment, at Loreto convent, Lucknow. Gary sent me the pictures of the house he had designed and built. It had skylights in each room and large French windows overlooking greens. Snapshots from his work and personal life were on my mantle. An extended family across the ocean. He had married Anne and had a son 'Jonathon' – more pictures.

I married a fighter pilot and moved to a different fighter base each year. Those were days of arranged marriages. It did not mean that we did not meet the person prior to marrying, we did. But the adage that 'you love the man you marry, and not marry the man you love' was prevalent in traditional Indian society. Girls usually married anywhere from eighteen to twenty. That was considered the right age. I came home from teaching at the convent school to see my house being decorated and sweetmeats on the table. I asked the housekeeper "Who is coming over?"

She informed me that I was getting engaged. I knew then. The issue I had dodged for so long and refused suitors was confronting me. I had met my future husband and heard him recite Ogden Nash poems with relish at the family dinner the night before. Was I prepared to marry at that point and him? I do not know, do not remember. My silence was taken as a shy 'yes.' A sign of what was to come. A different world! A world where I learnt a lot, stepped out of my shell and into the Air-Force world of adventure and frequent change. Air-Force became my family.

Gary was consistent with his correspondence. He sponsored a writer's correspondence course from New York and sent me a subscription of the 'Time' magazine as a gift. The greatest surprise was the unasked sponsorship form, he sent me. It lay with the tickets in my drawer for years. I would look at it and wonder how difficult it was to separate myself from my circumstance and travel. There was too much going on in life. I did not realize that I was the architect of it. Love of going to States became a wish for future.

The world I lived in emotionally and geographically was quite different from the one I had in mind. I had not read the signs, paid little heed to the nagging voice within me, which was pointing me in a different direction. Fear had overshadowed love and the clarion call to 'follow my bliss.' Being on the move all the time, Gary's consistent friendship and his letters kept me grounded and abreast of world news. In return I wrote to him about Indian texts, happenings, culture and more. He was into Gandhi, his vegetarianism and non-violence. Deeply entrenched in the hectic life of the Airforce and demands of domesticity, I lost track.

Then a sign appeared – a dream that all was not well with Gary. I had not heard from him for some time, and had a nagging feeling all was not well, I should write to him. I knew he was having domestic and health problems. Perhaps this was a precursor of what was to come. The story gets poignant here. As his situation worsened, physical signs of helplessness crept in. He had pneumonia and stayed under his electric blanket. I had never heard of these in India. Feeling concerned and curious I wrote to him.

As I got ready to mail the letter, I heard a knock at the door. It was the postman. He brought me two letters from Bethany, New York on the same day. Enclosed in one was another sponsorship form. There was a sense of urgency in his request for me to sign and send them. The next letter was from his wife Anne informing me of his demise. It contained a beautiful card, an invitation for his funeral with details of the ceremony. Strange that they would come simultaneously. Feeling devastated, I redid the envelope with a heartfelt letter of condolence, accompanied by Gary's sponsorship form. I then walked to the post office. It was a long and reflective walk and has been ever since. I call it my 'memory walk.' The mention of New York stirs memories of Gary.

Choices Versus Chances

"Two roads diverged in the wood; I took the one less travelled and that has made all the difference."

– Robert Frost

The pandemic had struck the world. I was detected with cancer. Afraid to go in for the surgery after my sister lost her life to it, I put it out of my mind. Being alone and with the responsibility of a daughter with a disability due to post surgery complications, I worried. Then as if God sent me a sign by way of Brian who stood firm by my side assuring me all would be well if I did go in for it. I did and at the operation trouble I remember there was this faith he had shown in me that I carried with me. I thought, *if I became all right and had a second chance what would I do?* My answer was 'give unconditional love, use my time on earth wisely.' The anaesthetic began to work and when I woke up the surgery was over. He had become a muse – a messenger.

Deeming the journey in this world is a forest with forks in the road, we choose where to turn. Or is the path already chosen? Are these choices, conscious or unconscious? Where do they come from? Why do they stymie us? When I reach a fork in the road, I remember three deities. The Creator, the Preserver and the Destroyer. They are three dimensions of the One: Brahma, Vishnu and Shiva. It is reassuring to note that no matter how vulnerable and wrong we are, there is someone looking after us, guiding us, will be there in the end. This is made known by signs we will find when we look carefully, have faith, hope and charity.

There is a learning curve in each choice we make. When we interpret this, we turn tables, perceive circumstance differently and see a new horizon. Perhaps this is what my father was trying to show me. A path of inner growth! My father understood my artistic and creative bent of mind. He prevailed upon my career choice and life partner choice. My love and respect for him made me follow suit. Being financially independent and employed as a high school teacher, I could have gone my way. This would have hurt him. I loved my parents too much to hurt them and went in for an arranged marriage.

When he arranged marriage for me, I was in two minds. In India they say "Love the man you marry; not marry the man you love." This was in olden times. Times had changed. Love marriages were frequent, so were divorces. In a country and at a time when dating was not common and convent schools were all same sex schools, one hardly got a chance to interact with boys other than at work. Parents became match makers. One day I come from teaching and see the house being decorated and sweet meats on the table. I ask the housekeeper who is coming. She answers: "You are getting engaged."

I recalled the evening before a fighter pilot had come home for tea and while talking about his adventures, he quoted Ogden Nash a lot. My father loved the wit and humor and when he asked me, "How did you like him?" I was quiet. This silence was taken as an acquiescence. Having refused so many suitors, I suppose my joint family thought it was time they had me betrothed and silence became a sign of approval. I had no regrets. Giving in was simpler than giving up on values of respect. How signs were interpreted and how signs were comprehended changed the course of one's life. Many a depressed person is not ill. He did not allow life to express itself and snubbed the cigarette before it was lit. Did not acknowledge the opening bud of potential and love, crushed it in himself and another out of fear

Feelings become a sign. Watch your feelings. Some things seem right. They leave you with a sense of peace. Others feel so wrong, even if they are listed as right. They leave you worn out. How do you choose right from wrong but by using the index of your feeling.

Fear is lack of courage and love is dare. There is risk involved in both cases. We take a chance with either. We grow or diminish accordingly. One cannot calculate to the decimal which is right or what the end will be. AS long as we have the capacity to love, we fulfill our mission, our dream, and give the world what we have come to deliver. Remember He is channeling through us, hence judging us or anyone is futile. Building bonds of humanity is key. And this can be done by reading signs, loving, and giving, not by denial and fear. The latter speaks in many languages of chance and choice. Each choice is a responsibility, and each chance is an opportunity. Amidst these lies free will.

The question is: When faced with choices, how do we make them? Gut feeling? Inner voice? Instinct? What will be the reason or emotion in making our choice? These questions pop up in making choices consciously. What about unconscious choices? Signs tell us they are made for us. How are they made? Can we alter our fate? Questions such as these plague minds that are exposed to eastern, western cultures, are thinking minds and reasoning minds. The believer in them be they scientist or other knows the vast field of the unknown. Fear props up when we begin to peel the layers. Not if we peel it with love. Then belief sets in. We can be wrong but at least we have not let fear get in the way and given life our best shot.

Sometimes I feel, we distance ourselves to observe the phenomena, to read the signs and interpret them, clairvoyance sets in. WE are led to 'The Way' – People do not just turn up; they are sent to us. Everything happens for a reason. Those things that are beyond reason fall in the realm of faith. We encounter people and work with them as souls to reach our destination. Love is calibration of energy when we meet such people, it awakens feeling that seems like a calling. Either we evolve and are transformed or if they ditch us, we get into a stupor of why and how trust was broken. Was it really love? What we forget is that love is giving and the person we love is not necessarily calibrated in energy and consciousness. We met for a purpose of raising consciousness.

There is fear when relationships do not work out. These can be personal or professional relationships. Fear devours the feeling of love. Signs of these are seen in silos, non communication, blame games, judgement of the other, trying to restrict communication, compartmentalize another and customize the relationship. Deep sadness follows when this happens. The signs of this are ill health, loss of interest and lustre and like a flower without water, the person begins to fade, while the other walks away without any remorse focussing on his narcissist self. Is it really worth the heartache to break trust?

When people stay fogged in the world of transactions, they seldom read the signs of oncoming events in their life, its passing, it's telling them something. Regrets are futile after that. 'You can't make a dead man alive' goes the saying.

Man chasing his hat.

Upon seeing the gale blow hard in Galway, the old man chased his hat. Each time he ran after it, the wind blew it further. This happened a couple of times. "The proverbial old man after his hat" said some interns at the med school. Old man chasing his hat became a sign for Madeline to choose her partner for life. Joe Daly removed himself from the group, ran up to the hat caught it and gave it to the old man. This made an impression on Madeline. It helped her decide who her life partner would be. It became an incident which actualized into a marriage

Our partners play a big role in determining our fate. Their vision and values influence us. Madeline made the right choice. She saw and comprehended the sign of loving kindness in the man she was to marry. And she stood up for love.

Love is a journey not a destination. In the battle between fear and love, the latter wins. Its effects are rewarding as they make us see the unseen and know the unknown. **You do not reach love. You become love**. It is the path you tread on. You become the path. It is a tumultuous sky. No one knows when it will pour. We do not plan to fall in love. It happens imperceptibly. Sky changes colour.

Rumi, the sagacious poet says: **"The day you were born, a ladder was set up to help you escape the world."** *Where is the ladder?* I always wondered, till I discovered that **struggle** was the ladder to 'learning and transcendence.' Overcoming fears cast by illusion and deceptions made it easier to cross over. I saw signs mitigating uncertainty, clarifying meaning and being resplendent in many ways. Most disorders of the body and mind are indicative signs of what is happening in our lives. Successes and failures are signs too. When we look beyond fear, we see the truth about ourselves. But do we want to see the truth? Can we handle it?

Diagnostic Signs

"It is not more surprising to be born twice than once.
Everything in nature is resurrection."

– Voltaire

Summer vacations had just ended. It was 1977. Boarders at Loreto Convent had returned to school. There was a buzz of enthusiasm and activity. I was on dormitory duty post-dinner. While taking rounds, I came across an interesting scene. One of the grade four students Mary, was standing on her bed circled by friends, performing a cabaret, shedding her clothes before she flung her nightie on. The other girls around her gaped. They wondered what she was doing, by undressing in public.

Stymied, some called her bad, others were tickled. When I stopped to watch the scene, Mary said: "You know when I went to my father's hotel in Kathmandu for summer holidays, I saw a cabaret every day. This is how they did it."

"Welcome to the Real World," words had hardly escaped my mouth when the students began repeating: 'real world – real world – real world!' The soundscape must have resounded through the dormitory, as Sr. Mary, a British nun known for her terse and dry wit, a terror to girls, came in with hurrying steps. Both the Mary's looked at each other. I witnessed a Biblical scene. The young Mary – 'Mary Magdalene' throwing off her nightie and baring herself – while the crowd cheered, and Sr. Mary watching her disapprovingly. Both were red in the face.

For me it became a sign of the real world in which the parents lived, and an artificial world to which they sent their prodigy or vice versa. It was also a sign of how our environment affects our behaviour. Like a carbon paper. Images and experiences affect young minds by imprints. The latter play an important role in later years. At first, we make the memory, then we become the memory.

My interest in signs of the spirit led me to investigate the spirit's role in each circumstance. Suffering from typhoid and its relapse, I had grown weak. Doctors had given up hope. Some saw these signs and said, "It was a matter of time." Senior Cambridge examination were a week away. I had no intention of lagging behind. Though weak in body I made my intention known to the universe, as everyone around prayed for recovery.

On the night that the doctor had termed as 'critical,' I felt a presence of light wake me. I woke up with a start. It was so brilliant that I could not look up.

A second chance at life was given to me. Wanting to record the moment, lest I forget it, I scribbled a verse on the back of a mini–Oxford Dictionary lying on the side table: "Dressed in light you come to me, your thought is so restorative, how much more will your company be." I went to sleep after that.

Next morning, when the doctor visited me, he was happily surprised. He thought medicine, had done the job. I knew the Spirit had intervened. My temperature had gone back to below normal. This was a sign that I was well. My parents were ecstatic. I was happy I could now write my examinations. The dictionary with my scrawl still lay beside my bed. The universe had come through. Typhoid had been defeated at a time when the only cure for it was penicillin.

Upon insistence, my father agreed to take me to write the examinations with no preparation. On the last day of the examination, his car broke down in the middle of nowhere, at an early hour. The sisters at the convent were truly kind and helpful, yet rules are rules, and the hall door would close on time. I was worried and cried out for help. I saw a bird fly past me, as birds do in the early hours of the morning. I prayed. Shortly, I saw a family friend come by on a scooter. His residence was nowhere near our house. It was too early to go to the office. He stopped by and offered me a ride. On the way to school, he told me that a thought came to him that morning, to visit me and see how I was doing. He acted on that thought.

I asked him, "What time?" "Early," he said. It was the time the car had broken down and I had cried out for help in prayer, with faith and belief so this last examination would go through. **People do not come to us. They are sent.**

Upon reaching, I found Sr. Wilfrid waiting for me. She accompanied me to the examination hall. The history paper read: "It took the entire British Empire to keep Gandhi in poverty" Elucidate. I read the question. It did not require memory of dates. Thank God it was an opinion piece. Words flowed. I was surprised what power, will, intent can have. Now and then, I would look up at Sr. Wilfrid and find her smiling down at me in appreciation. She was a sign of loving kindness and strength that kept my fingers moving. The spirit energizes and moves both the body and the mind. Without it, one limps and is listless. I learnt a lot from the I.B.V.M. sisters and am grateful for their kindness.

Signs appeared when I immigrated to Canada alone, knowing no one. All I had was the intent that I had to give my daughter a last shot and see what I could do to salvage her lost eye. Giving up home, marriage, security, leaving behind a promising career, parents and family was not easy. I imagined I would be back soon. It did not happen that way. All along there were signs. For example, after my post grad classes at U of T. and my work in the evening, I passed several stores at Yonge and Summerhill before turning into my street. One evening I saw a sign "Volunteers needed." Barbara Hall was running for Mayor. I stepped in to fill out the application. I so missed my family especially in the evenings that it seemed a perfect fit to help out during this time. I signed up. Here I met so many interesting people and learnt a lot. What is more I made friends with Barbara Hall, Dr. Bennett and others.

Being trapped in the bank of Montreal when I went in to get some money from the ATM, I did not know how to operate the door. It had opened when I got in but would not when I tried again. New to the country, I racked my brains. What was I doing wrong? It was a Sunday morning. The bank was closed. I had no cell phone. Few people on the street. No one looked left or right. They simply walked past the bank. I so needed help and could not imagine being trapped in the bank.

I tried to catch the attention of several pedestrians but to no avail. Then I paused and prayed for a sign. I blue dot, a big button next to me. I was wondering if that had to be pressed when I saw a man from outside come to my rescue. His name was Mark and he worked for the television. I thanked him over a cup of tea at the café nearby. It was so interesting to note that he had me speak about Medicinal plants and cooking at a university health class later. This added to my diverse experience, and I made an acquaintance.

I began to look for signs when stranded. Being aware is essential for a newcomer, as there is so much to learn. I remember Philip saying when I was appointed to lead the Research and Development unit of India's school board. "Just look for signs, be aware." His words held good. I sensed a lot and reflected. The intent being to help out and better communicate. It paid off.

Advice at the right time and the right moment goes a long way. It comes through the mouth of babes too. We just need to self correct all the time. As we peel the onion, we cry sometimes. As we proceed on the spiritual path, calendars, dates, and time gets erased. Experiences and how they made us feel take precedence. We base our memories on experience, till experience becomes a memory to guide us and be a sign of learning and wisdom. The law of association between the event and the feeling it created becomes predominant. Each experience is a learning experience. Each person is a teacher. This includes children. We have simply to read the signs to understand their love, their patience with us, their fear of disobeying and more. We learn when we open our minds and our hearts. I learnt a lot from children, students and humble folk who wear no badges other than their goodwill and willingness to serve.

In the early 1980s my husband a fighter pilot. was posted at a fighter base in northern India. Three pilots were selected to go to Russia. They were to fly MiG 23 fighter aircraft from Frunze, Russia. He was one of them. All three wives left behind were pregnant. The men were supposed to return in three to four months. That did not happen. Weather conditions and technical details prevented their timely return. My neighbour Tara and I took our constitutional walks together. She had a two-year-old boy and I a daughter of the same age. Both of us were expecting our second child a week apart. Tara went in for delivery ten days prior to me at the military hospital and returned with a son, to tell her story. "On the delivery table, a nurse addressed as sister, scolded me for dirtying her white apron. Then another nurse walked in. She was fresh and young, seemed a trainee or an apprentice. I was having my pains when the first sister H.G. said to the new nurse, "My time is up. My duty done. Now you take over."

"Was this a change of guard in the middle of a delivery?" Tara said.

She begged the officious H.G. to please finish the job, as the new nurse said that it was her first day in the delivery room to independently handle it.

After much reluctance, H.G. stayed, grumbling, and complaining, as if she were doing Tara a favour. "Beware of H.G. when you go in," Tara said.

My time came. It was anxious who it would be. Reading the name plates of the sisters, I spotted H.G. She was coming towards me. Detecting arrogance from her manner and walk, I remembered what Tara had said. 'Beware!' The sign appeared.

"May I see the doctor, please?" I could not help asking.

"No, he is not necessary. I will take over." She was determined to decide my fate. I got more determined not to let her. As she stepped out of the room, my pains sharpened. There were no Tylenols administered. Nothing like a labor pain. I had to get the doctor's attention. Tara's warning kept repeating itself. 'Avoid H.G. if you can.'

My fear: 'What if she deserts me in the middle of the procedure? What could I do?' Each time I tried to call out, labour pains would stop me. There was no call bell. To get the attention of the medicos, I picked up a huge vase beside my bed and flung it at the door. Shattering sound! Hurrying steps. They sounded like H.G.'s. Sure, H.G. came in but with her came in the doctor. By the time they wheeled me in, my son was born. A ten-pound baby! I was twenty-two then and had never done this before, to attract attention. A strategy that spontaneously came to my rescue saved us both. Deliverance!

Forty days later, when I took my new-born son for a check up, I was in for another surprise. These were winter months and we lived in a large bungalow with umpteen windows in each room. They creaked and did not close properly. No central heating. Electric heaters were there in each room. Power would go off frequently. Then it became a 'blow hot, blow cold' situation. I could hear a wheezing sound from his lungs. The doctor checked him, shook his head, and said: "You have brought him too late."

"What do you mean by 'too late'?" I asked.

"We'll admit him into the I.C.U. and put him on oxygen, you can get admitted too with him and watch him for forty-eight hours. That is the best I can do," he said.

That was the most trying time of my life. He was on a ventilator. I prayed unceasingly as I watched him. I could not fathom this to be the end. Time was racing. So were my tears. I watched mortality spin its yarn. The nurses in their cursory way would ask each other, "bed no. 5 empty – patient dead." Aghast at this stark reality at twenty-two, I tried to fathom life at many portals. Pushing away icy hands of death came with faith and incessant prayer. It was time for the Spirit to intervene. **When left with no hope, He became my hope, certainty, and reality. I saw a sign and met it with faith.** In the middle of the night, someone suggested, I go to a Sufi saint's shrine a kilometer away barefoot. He was a Muslim 'peer' who answered prayers. I was not a Muslim. Yet, it was a moment of crisis. Faith mattered, religious diversity did not. There was no room for disbelief. I got going…

The one branch I held on to was of unswerving faith, hope and love. These mitigated fear.

Leaving him in the care of the nursing staff at the I.C.U. I ran barefoot to the shrine. This was a km. away from the hospital. Feeing the gravel beneath my feet – the empty road ahead in the dark night, I threw care and safety to the winds. This was what love looked like for a mother whose son was struggling for breath.

Soon, I stood under a large banyan tree whose roots went into the ground, then came up next to the shrine. Hands folded with faith and fervour. The 'Peer baba'[4] who answered everyone's prayers must save my son now. Leaves rustled in the cold night breeze. Falling on my knees, I begged for his life. At that point it did not matter to me whether he was a Muslim, a Hindu, or a Christian. All that mattered was—saving a life! Peer baba helped humans in distress. I called out to the universe for awakening life, saving Manik. Running back like a bull charged with passion, I felt the rush of warm blood gushing through me. Intuition was telling me something. Fear and faith combat. What was I going to observe upon return?

Upon entering the I.C.U. I found doctors standing by his bed. Some of the pilot officers from the squadron had come in. My eyes went straight to the tubes they had inserted in him. They were taken off. This scared me. I got closer. My faith held me. The doctor looked at me. 'Miracle!' he exclaimed. "He is breathing." Divine intervention! Faith over medicine, or both. **Love had triumphed over fear.**

"We could have driven you – why barefoot?," the officers asked. "You will not understand this," I said. This sacrifice and earnestness were needed. I had

---

[4] saint

to do this. I was so grateful to the Supreme power for having saved my son's life. Love conquered the physical catastrophe. The officers returned a month later from Frunze. A lifetime had been lived. A new life had been born. A life had been saved.

Predictive Signs

"Paul rose from the ground and with open eyes – he saw nothing."
– St. Luke in acts about St. Paul

There is no one way to interpret signs as they are culturally different. For example, the swastika in Hindus is a sacred sign and in Nazi Germany had a very different connotation. Similarly, the serpent is a sacred sign of Shiva in Hinduism and a temptation in the Garden. History tells us that when Lord Krishna was born there was lightening messaging the birth of Krishna. Locks on the prison doors opened. His father Vasudeva carried him in a basket through the Yamuna River to a safe portal at his brother's house beyond Yamuna. It was pouring heavily, and a cobra snake shielded the basket. The Cobra became a protector of the divine. His presence posited safety from hail and thunder in the choppy waves of the Yamuna.

I relate an experience that altered the pattern of my life: It is was busy afternoon at the India International Center, New Delhi. I am hosting a national competition to select a speaker from the I.C.S.E. schools. The student would participate in the P.E.S.A.[5] competition in Melbourne, Australia.

Dr. Ray Maddocks had asked for India to participate. "Indians speak good English," he says. Yet, the students who spent effort and energy in learning the language did not have venues to showcase it. Here was one international venue. How could I walk past it?

I met Ray in my capacity as the Head of R.D.C.D. at the I.C.S.E. in New Delhi. Within a few months, I became aware of Australia's international programs, and how I could introduce and engage Indian students in this. Excited in collaborating and opening doors for schools, I agreed to participate in the Plain English-Speaking competition held in Melbourne in June 1997.

---

[5] Plain English-Speaking competition set up by Australia as an Asia Pacific Venture.

Little did I know what this would involve. Nobody was on board at the office. It was responsibility. It meant getting out of one's comfort zone to take responsibility and who would undertake this?

I had given my word to Ray and was convinced that Indian students should go ahead and showcase their learning on an international platform. So, I acted out of the courage of my conviction. I acted alone. I knew there would be dissent, it would not be easy, yet I took that one step based on my belief in myself, the conviction to make this opportunity come alive for Indian students. Ray became a sign of providing this opportunity. Others joined me as the project evolved. That first step was mine. It arose out of giving legs to faith. Someone had to open that door. The mantle fell on me. Schools were ecstatic.

Fundraising, communications, event management, air tickets, accommodations etc. were challenges to be surmounted. I was not going to be defeated by these. Believing that the best help is at the end of one's arm, I began knocking at doors. Qantas Airlines said they needed advanced notice to consider the tickets, there was no government support, none from the education portfolio I held. So, I went to corporations. Coca Cola and Pepsi came forward with free drinks and caps for participating students, some other friends and corporations brought about ads. for the brochure I planned to publish. In a short time, I had just about enough with the help of the community that cared after running a twelve-hour marathon each day. Finally, Ray flew in, twenty-eight schools participated from the twenty-five states. Arrangements were made for the stay of students courtesy Y.M.C.A. New Delhi. In brief the event was a huge success with excellent speakers and judges, members from the French and Australian High Commission attended. All this, at a time when I was immigrating to Canada. May 8/1997 was the day of the event and a week later I was to fly. My visa which lay in the drawer for a year. It was about to expire. I wanted to explore the possibility for my daughter in Canada where there was socialistic medicine.

Despite the uncertainty and rush, I stood committed. India was represented in the Asia Pacific competition in 1997. What is more, the winner of the India competition won the Asia Pacific competition too. I had paid for his ticket.

This news reached me, when I was in Toronto, Canada. Happy at having opened doors, it turned out to be a labour of love with no strings attached. That was the secret of its success. I had labored with all my resources and strength believing in the cause turning apprehension, hesitation, and fear into an opportunity for Indian students in Australia.

Love honoured translates into action. In the break between the sessions, I watched the students at lunch time, chatted with them casually. A warm feeling came over me. A sense of achievement.

In the corridor, I was approached by a six-foot-tall 'Swami.'[6] He greeted me with a 'namaste.' Returning his greeting, I asked him if he knew me.

"No," he said, "but I recognize you and have something to tell you – something I sensed. Can we meet after the program?"

"Sure," I replied and got busy. Before leaving, I remembered the man who wanted to see me and say something. He was still waiting in the corridor. Quickly, I hastened my steps curious. He got up and signalled me to a vacant chair. I sat down in anticipation.

"I saw a sign when I saw you," he said.

"Hmm," I thought, *never heard that before.*

"Do I have your permission to tell you?" he asked.

"Yes," I was very eager to know.

"You come from a yogi family, in your last birth you lived in a royal family in Manali. Have you ever been to Manali?" he asked.

"No. Never! I heard it is a beautiful hill station, referred by some as 'Valley of the Flowers' and Kulu, the adjacent district as 'Valley of the Gods.'"

"Well," he said, "you loved horses and against the family tradition, you fell in love with your trainer and eloped with him. He is your present-day husband."

"Is he fond of horses?" he asked me.

"Yes," I said, "he is an avid rider. He even owns a horse and keeps him on his airfield."

"Well, you went back after that, to your family, to set things right."

I looked at him, wondering *why he was telling me all this.*

"Listen carefully," he said.

"You will not stay long here in India – your destiny is in Canada."

I thought it was Australia, as I was working with Dr. Ray Maddocks, in a joint venture 'Victoria International Services,' to represent Australian Education Institutes in India.

---

[6] Holy man

"No," he said – soon you will be leaving."

What was he suggesting?

The unconscious has its way of emerging. That night I had a dream. I was climbing a hill with certitude and came upon a broken and aged red brick boundary wall. It was dilapidated. I went around it to the gate. Entering it, I saw an old charpoy.[7] Lying on it was an old woman. Trying to sit up and peer through her round framed glasses, she said; "You have returned Bublee?"

"I knew you would come some day. They thought I had lost my mind chasing the dead. But I knew, in my heart I felt, that you would come some day. And you have come." She smiled a toothless smile. I knew then. The love in her eyes was contagious. It stirred a memory. I wanted to hug her and tell her how much I missed her. "Look what has happened to the place." She pointed to the tall grass and to the dilapidated mansion. She then clapped her hands. An old man with a bent back came out of the building. "You have grown so old Munshi," I said. He looked at me keenly. "Bublee-" Recognition lit his eyes. There was disbelief in them. The picture of a ten-year-old playing marbles flashed across my mind. His eyes had the same mischievous look of win and run.

This dream came two decades plus when I met the swami – a memory button got triggered. I have been in Canada for that many years. Signs indeed!

In a similar vein my friend Suman Rao, the wife of the Commanding officer at Air-Force station, Halwara, Panjab, told a gathering at a social event, how a certain Cdr. Green in Bangalore, had predicted her husband would be posted to Bangkok, Thailand as an Air Attaché. Even the date of his posting turned out to be correct. "You must see Cdr. Green on 53 Brigade Road" she said.

The thought stayed in my mind. A few years later we were in Bangalore. While my family went to see a film, I went directly to 53, Brigade Rd. In an old villa with green creepers, wearing an unkempt kurta pajama sat Cdr. Green, an old, bearded man looking more like a saint than a naval commander.

He greeted me warmly as if he had been waiting for ages for me to arrive. Holding my right hand, he said: "I am holding the hand of an old soul." I was twenty-five then. I knew nothing about old and young souls, except that I had one.

---

[7] cot

Then he asked me to pick a Tarot card from the pack. This I did. He made me pick several of them. Then he paused to read them. I was astonished at what all he told me. There was an energy flow in the room. He went on with dates, places I would visit, children, and how they would shape up. He had to stop. Some of it was a foreboding. I tried not to think of it at age twenty-five. Some of it came to pass as the years scrolled.

When fear was ripped, disbelief dismantled, then love in all its splendour, revealed the crystal ball. I was touching unknown shores in faith.

Religious Signs

"The Porcupine is a sign of the Prophet's soul----hardship makes the soul emerge."

– Rumi

The tapestry of religions is woven with the cross, the Om, the Mandela, the Crescent Moon and more. Each displays a pattern of thought, an interpretation, a connection to the other religion. Each symbolizes a story, a myth, a ritual, and a congregation. The **'Biblical Seven Signs'** in the Gospel of John, talk about the miracles performed by Jesus: For example, showing his power over death by waking Lazarus from the dead, over nature by walking on water and so forth. These were not performed for personal gain but representative of God's power bestowed upon him.[8] He also asked the blind if they wanted to see. Blind here refers to those with eyes who refuse to see, to take cognizance. There must be a need, a vacuum before it is filled. Grace understands this. We seldom do.

A rendezvous with the divine is a personal living religion to me with humanity at its core and seeing another as myself, seeing the divine in each creation. Everything is connected and imbued with meaning we are yet to discover.

Signs **reveal the hidden truths** and decode what is not apparent. They restore belief, can be spontaneous or evoked by a ritual. Signs can come from the five senses, the sixth sense, one's culture, intuition, dreams and more.

Cultures are interwoven because all experience reflects the human experience in a human form. As for the function of signs – they mitigate

---

[8] M.C. Tenney

uncertainty, clarify meaning and add dimension beyond meaning. Saints and prophets were called to their vocation. They read the signs. They heard the voices. They listened. They performed. It is no different now. People still hear voices. Sometimes they get branded as 'Schizophrenics.'

Our society is so bent upon labelling, segregating, and categorizing because of the medical bias of differentiating science from religion. Yet, it is new experience that teaches us new ways of communicating, relating, and revering the sacred in us and in another.

Where would Einstein, Newton, and other inventors stand today when labelled? The sign of the falling apple from the tree helped Newton discover the law of gravity. It is in those moments of idle awareness that we discover. Fear blocks creativity.

Sacred space is the most important piece of real estate. We cannot buy nor sell sacred space. We can cultivate it nurture it, protect it from being judged and discarded. Often, perceptions, lack of courage come in the way. Lovers want to be accepted by the larger piece of humanity. There is no such thing as 'what will people say.' There is no such body as people. Each is an individual with their own psyche, perceptions, attitudes and more. When unconditional love is subjected to criticism, evaluation, jealousy and more, by one of the two it recoils. It is of the Spirit.

We seldom realize this because of our past experiences. If we have not experienced unconditional love, we think it fluky, unreal, in the mind. And discard it thus to suit a more tangible reality. "What is tangible if not the intangible made real?' The spirit invades the body, and we have life. The Spirit leaves the body, and we have death. When the Spirit is in the body and acknowledged by another spirit it gets rejuvenated and shines. When ignored, judged, and categorized it suffers. This is the crux of love and fear. It is what you pay attention to, that becomes real.

"We do not need a new religion. We need a new experience," says, Allen Watts. It is experiences that teach, shape, and make us who we are. Without them we cannot connect. Yet, we are not open to them. They promote meaningful conversations. We are afraid to face the truth. Scared of being our best and facing our reality. Hence, we dismiss signs that are not in accordance with our expectations. Ignorance may be bliss, but not in this case. It becomes an impediment. This can be removed by 'education of consciousness.' The latter can be imbued with meaning and stories, not just deliver facts and figures. Did Jesus not teach with parables? There were signs in the parables for us to interpret. These have become icons imbued with meaning for generations.

Phenomenology acquires a meaning etched in the reality of our beings. There is no **one** way of interpreting a sign. For example, water may signify cleanliness, but may not be clean. In her book, *Significance of Signs*, Kim Bearden writes, "open mindedness is essential for signs to appear – they come in spontaneously or upon evocation." They are a representational medium used in business, as much as in Divinity. "Triad is a sign of balance, harmony, wisdom. friendship, piety, and peace. Hence the signifier, the sign and the signified – the meaning represented by the sign are rooted in social and cultural meaning. They do not have their own essence but are relational." – Berger A.A., 'The Science of Signs.'

The **Mandela** is the Buddhist sign of **balance**. Meditating on it is a constant reminder of maintaining balance in eating, drinking, working out, sleeping and more.

Departure Signs

Departures are never final. We carry the people we leave behind in our hearts.

Schwester[9] Miriam was an Austrian nun, who taught me German, at St. Mary's Covent, after school hours. She went into the depth of linguistics, their roots, phonetics, cultures, and mentored me. I have long forgotten German as a language but remember the anecdotes, the spirit and her.

I learnt about her fleeing from Nazi Germany, about the ordeals people had to face and more. It was first-hand knowledge. I met Schwester Miriam while I was completing my Senior Cambridge and later when I was teaching at St. Mary's Convent. We became friends and discussed everything under the sun after the lesson was over, including my would-be suitors. She crocheted a lace table cover for me as a wedding gift.

I was touched by her consistency and presence in my life. We continued to correspond for several years until one day I received a sign – a letter from her that ended in **"One never knows when one says goodbye for the last time."** This sentence hit a nerve. I wrote her back. There was no response for a month.

---

[9] Sister in German

I prayed she was well. No communication from her worried me. I wrote to the convent only to be told that Schwester Miriam had died. It was the day the letter had arrived in my mailbox. The letter she wrote was a goodbye letter, a sign of her departure. She wished me 'goodbye' before she finally left. I did not understand then. I do now.

In the same vein, while I was returning to the university, I saw the look on my grandpa's face. It was his final goodbye. He had taught me to perceive without words being spoken, to understand without being told. I learnt lessons in sensitivity and comprehension. His eyes followed me as the car moved away. I had a hunch that the gaze that followed my departure, would become a goodbye gaze. In a few months it became from a living grandpa to a fond memory. His time was over in one place and beginning in another. *Do people we love communicate their departure?* I wondered.

Vibrations

"Everything in life is a vibration."

– Albert Einstein

What are halos around the heads of sacred people but vibrational energies that heal us, calm us and speak to us. These vibrations can be both positive and negative. The question is, 'What kind of energy are you inviting?' The mundane transactional or the deep transformational. The signs are explicit in each case. They are not comfortable on either side. Whenever there is growth there is discomfort whether at puberty biologically speaking or a new learning here cognition is involved. There are initial failures before one grasps the vibration and integrates it. There is a deserve before desire. Hence, vibrations like insights, strong attractions are mysteries revealed to some not all.

Once you feel these do not deny them. They are more than human intelligence. In them are seeds of the Unseen and the Unknown.

The big bang theory tells us that the world began with a vibration. Hinduism tells us of Shiva bowing his conch shell and its vibrations set the world in motion. Christianity speaks of Genesis and signs.

What vibrations and frequency are we living at? Higher, lower, medium is the determining factor of energy calibrating. A 'yes' is more powerful than a 'no.' It is the frequency at which one sets one's mind. Set it to a positive frequency and vibrations like inspiration, the Muse, the messages from another world will flood their light on your ignorance and dispel darkness bringing clairvoyance.

This is the purpose of life to calibrate energy by 'Right Associations.' We mistakenly consider association to be based in status quo. It is not. It is vibrational and contagious. You may be living in another continent and catch the vibrations from a quite different place. This is how distant healing takes place, this is how prayers reach the Supreme and we connect.

When we draw fiscal boundaries and open the ledger to make entries of those, we associate with seldom do energies calibrate – transactions do. People get stiff on other seats and glued to their perceptions. We feel the vibrations of another, of nature, of things to come, of storms in the teacup. And when the cup in our hands shakes, we are aroused to love or to fear. The world arose out of the vibrations from Shiva's conch shell. According to Hindu mythology.

Vibrations can be positive or negative. We are not always aware of them and wonder why despite our best-efforts things do not go right. vibrations are constantly sending messages. These are signs which can be sensed. We need to calibrate our energies. Our vibration is our energy

Yet we stay transfixed in our perceptions. They define our actions. We seldom understand unconditional love, Grace, or the nature of gifting. To us it is material. We forget in the material body is a spirit. It is all powerful. Yet, we squash it, admonish it in us and in another. There is a difference in knowing and doing. In this gap lies suffering, transition and more. When we are in this gap of being misunderstood by our words, deeds, and thoughts, we are in pain. We strive to reach out to the lover outside – it does not work. The lover has closed his mind. His spirit is locked up and is handcuffed. Silenced he wavers like Hamlet. Inside his mind are phantoms that rise and fall. Hence, he speaks from two sides of his mouth trying to please all. Keeping apprehensions at bay he can speak his truth which is universal truth. There is no duality in Truth. It is revelation, it is reality, there is hope, there is evolution and there is freedom from suffering. How can one free another from suffering by closing doors of communication, mind, heart, spirit and staying handcuffed? Look at the signs, hear them, feel them and the answers will come. What is blocking you is the negatives. Positives will unfurl once you cross the hurdles of your mind.

Believing that we are but spokes of a wheel, all must work in harmony, to move collective consciousness, to grow, to complete the missing piece of the puzzle. Lucky are those, who have come across such souls in life and related to them. This results in evolution. But this does not always happen. The mind needs to be opened to reach to another and be reached by another.

Sometimes, we do not feel illumined or inspired, by those around us. There is struggle in finding inspiration, in finding the one, who will make us do, what we can do. He will show us our true beauty and walk us on the road to consciousness and happiness. It is the time to walk out of the thickets of negative energy and look at the sky.

Are we here to fill a void, created by not receiving and not giving love? Do we use material toys to put a lid on subjects that trouble us?

They say, 'fear is the key.'

I say, 'fear is the lock, love is the key.' Overused and much misunderstood, love needs to be revisited and redefined. Some fear it to be an intangible. It cannot be quantified and escapes definition. Yet, each heart craves it. It is not taught but a learned experience, like the butterfly struggling through the larvae. It becomes meaningful and beautiful, once it has crossed through the gate of fear.

Some get lost in transition, for lack of faith and patience. Faith is not just in love, but in the ones loved and in oneself. It is based on 'trust.' There is no judgement or expectation in it. Therefore, even God honours love. Man craves it. Found in the soul of each of us, love is abiding when true, eternal when unconditional.

And love is not just for the chronologically young. It does not necessarily imply sex. Parental love is not for being put on the back burner either. Siblings' love is not just friendship. Love of oneself is not necessarily self-indulgence. This rainbow of colour drips its essence through experience.

"The purpose of life is to be happy not comfortable."

– H.H. The Dalai Lama.

When we read the signs on peoples' faces, we understand why they act the way they do. Life needs **education of the heart, the mind, and the spirit to love and be loved.** Fear peeps from veiled uncertainty. Revelations are neither wrapped in gift paper, nor tied with strings. They are road signs to an evolving soul. Masks are just that – masks! True personality is revealed when the mask is off, the make up is off and the skin is bare. In unadulterated responses and expressions, we reveal our true selves spontaneously!

We create our reality both consciously and unconsciously by the choices 'we do not' make as much as those we do make. Cognitive abilities involved in making choices are attention, memory, executive functioning, language, visuospatial abilities and more. Each is linked to likes and dislikes, conditioning, and the law of attraction. Not making a choice, is also a choice. It is a sign of fear at times.

Fear of being wrong, ruining our image, leaving status quo, a job, a career that made us be the position we held are all signs of weakness not strength. They are a persona not a character. We evade to avoid consequences. It is just fear. Love explores. Fear deplores. Do we determine our choices or do our choices determine who we are and how far we will go? Conscious choices are those we make with our head. Unconscious choices are made by the subconscious and the unconscious. For example: falling in love – going a certain way – writing a certain verse.

Psychologists who have studied **Shamanism** in depth, regard this as 'a **therapeutic process.'**[10] Shamans do not usually choose their vocation but are called to it by signs, dreams, oracles and more. At first, we waste time, then time wastes us. In the fast-changing world, vulnerability is sometimes a strength. The paradigm is shifting, no matter which way you look at it. Strength is not out there in muscle power, be it financial muscle or otherwise. It is in strengthening the inner muscle of co-operation and collaboration. It is maintaining peace with oneself, despite contradictions and expectations of others, the change in calendar dates, people, attitudes, and issues.

It is extremely hard to do so, if we do not **reset** our inner compass. Most of us begin to feel vulnerable. Maintaining appearances becomes difficult. We feel stifled. Despite our best efforts, nothing works. Expectations go unmet. There is a disconnect. Living under the same roof becomes challenging. Many experience this and move away. Others stay put. Seldom do they explore how love could alter this fear and apprehension, especially during Covid-19. When and where will this paradigm shift take us? Is it individual or collective? Where do I go from here? How do I change? Who do I change into? What all do I change?

Questions sift through events, routines, and ordeals. We seek answers to quick fixes. I asked this to the audience while delivering a talk on 'Paradigm Shift.' The answers were thought provoking! Many heads turned. Many a man smiled. Many a lady burst out of her shell exclaiming – 'Is this it?' The response was disinhibiting. When I got a slip at the extempore speaking contest for universities in India, and it read 'Love is labor lost,' I was stymied. I

---

[10] Powers of Healing—Editors of Time—Life Books, Virginia

became aware of the energy in the room and took shelter drawing words from Shakespeare's tragedies. Little did I know I would live his realities and towards the end. feel love is not labor lost. Any experience that deepens understanding of human nature is neither labor nor is it lost. Sunlight streamed through the open window. Bathed in it, my spirit had risen to a crescendo of extempore speech, drawing knowledge from the light of 'consciousness.

Each one's life changes with oncoming realities, rewriting the script. We forget it is not yesterday. Time shifts. Black and white turn to grey. Accompanying emotions can be anxiety, apprehension, uncertainty. They soon become lenses through which we begin to see ourselves and others. Here we need to discern and feel not just look. to **let the spirit lead**. Yet, we hesitate, doubt tread unfamiliar ground beset with apprehensions. The spirit is intangible but palpable.

Spiritual Partnerships do not necessarily mean living under the same roof – having the same vocation – bearing children together. They are rooted in the psyche of the soul and the commitment to evolve together. The concept of the family has changed, the structure has evolved to extended families. The negative signs of non-acceptance are combated.

Spiritual evolution is showing signs of a collective evolution. Spiritual partnerships are happening more than ever. When imbued in the physical alone, we do not recognize this. Our intuitive self shows us signs. Often vibrations are felt in the vital physical. Denying them is futile. Accepting and learning from the experiences coming to us, discerning the messages is fulfilment. It is energizing and restorative, knowledge, and evolution.

I leave my house in Toronto to go to Barrie to teach. It is snowing lightly. I have no idea what I am to experience. By the time I reach Bradford there is a snowstorm. Visibility is zero. I roll down my window. Everything is white. I look for the road. It is a skating rink on the 400 Highway. Cars, Trucks, and fog lights are dim signs that show the way. Careful not to crash, I hold the steering wheel tightly, put on my flashers and drop the speed to 20. I see lights flashing behind me. It is a Cop car.

"Everything all right?" the lady cop asks.

"Figuring my way, why?"

"You have your flashers on and are driving at snail speed," she says.

"It's skiddy – my first time in a storm, I'm scared if I will ever reach my destination."

She understands and follows me. I am relieved to have a guide at this difficult period. Divine intervention! Faith took root in me, reminding me of a greater reality than reason.

Humanity is at risk because the important is placed at the discretion of the individual perception, not on the principles of humanity. Take the example of little things that make or mar a day. The difference between a smile and a frown. Smiles cost little but create much. They disintegrate differences and animosity. Helping, acknowledging, and responding never hurt one. But phantoms of the mind do hurt one and another.

Imagine a world filled with genuine people who stood by you, for you and trusted you, loved you unconditionally. What would be your response? Will you doubt their authenticity and turn your back? Will you have apprehensions: What does this person need from me? Many a jaded person might do just that. It is not the person who is jaded. It is his perception that needs awakening to a reality greater than himself. Each face is beautiful if we only see it thus. As I was taught: 'beauty lies in the eyes of the beholder.'

Vedic Prophecies

"Wild geese do not intend to cast their reflection; water has no mind to retain their image."

– Zen

The dove is a sign of peace, but it is not peace. People use it to send messages and also kill it as a prey for consumption. Signs are not what they predict. They are conveyor belts, agencies used for downloading mysteries and reaching them to other agencies. The world of signs may appear familiar, but it is more than meets the eye. This is why judging, measuring or assessing the harbinger of signs is not appropriate.

How does the Divine reach us by resurrection of Jesus? When the voiceless get a voice and are reached by prophets who have calibrated their energies, there is magic. People stand in awe. What had happened is that signs from another world powerful signs, also termed as Grace has stepped in reminding is: this is not all—Spirit supreme is connected and interrelated.

To be aware of phenomena at a higher level of vibrations, we need signs. **'Dying each day is surrender. Letting go is transient.'**[11] Thus, emptying oneself to a higher self is the kernel of our being. *Do we ever see the sign of death as a surrender, a transition, another journey?* I wonder, if we ever see the signs of life reverberate with the strings of nature – as if an orchestra were being conducted by a Maestro. For example, the reeds in the river, the swaying of trees in the wind, chirping of the birds are a part of us. Do we stop to smell the proverbial roses, look at the transcendental gaze of the deer, hear the song of the lark and wonder? It is this sense of wonder, that is being lost in the information age saturated with noise and 'know it all attitude.'

---

[11] Jiddu Krishnamurthy

In mythological ancient texts like 'Ramayana' for example, there are instances of man understanding the language of the animals and birds. The Indian epic is replete with such friendships. Hanuman is the monkey God who befriends Lord Rama and assists him in recovering Sita from Ravana.

If animals are so friendly, why do we eat them?

I saw peacocks perched on my garden her windowsill and the garden wall when mother was in her last moments on earth. They were sign of transformation and resurrection. Watching them gave her so much joy, it appeared she was following their message. They were communicating. I did not know I saw the most exotic birds I had never seen before come into my garden. Their chirping still haunts me. I did not know they were emissaries from heaven sent to relay a message.

Many great writers and poets, prophets and philosophers have fantasized death to be a lover. This takes fear away from death. Nostradamus mathematically reflected on his prophecies by meditating on time and events. He assigned meaning to them. The Buddhist **Mandela** is a sign of healing and transformation. One sign can however, mean different things in different cultures. For example, 'Swastika' is sacred to Hindus, but represents anti-Semitism to Germans.

Freud would say of signs: 'We see them. We do not see them. They are representative of meanings that go beyond the literal. They go into our unconscious and subconscious, connecting us to the supramental, the cosmos.' Towards the end of his life, **Sigmund Freud** began to connect the unconscious as a path to the Supernatural to the Divine. WE stand amidst history. It warns us. It builds awareness. Hurried steps lose sight of the pre-ordained – the mystery – the unexplored unconscious! The latter holds memories and future realms. The universe beckons us. We do not hear it, see its signs and carry on mindlessly stuck in our perceptions. When prophecies turn into reality, experiences acquire meaning and context. There are visible, auditory, and other signs. Prophecies or mystical happenings come from the Yogic term "Siddhis.' These were acquired after transcendence and prayer by holy men in India and elsewhere.

They are as old as the Vedas. The holy books of the Hindus talk about signs and synchronicities as revelations. There was no G.P.S. yet people traveled through thickets and forests. The G.P.S. was in signs, intuition, symbols and more. Education was not digital but pivotal. It was acquired by merit, ability, and reverence. It was not literacy. Leonardo Da Vinci was unlettered and had no formal education till age fourteen. This did not keep him from discoveries inventions and artistry. He saw sign all along and tried to read and know the unknowable. A sense of curiosity and embracing the uncertain helped him to discover and to create. It had to be earned and was not an entitlement.

Masters saw signs of potential in students before they took them on as apprentice. To be a student of a renowned master and sit at his feet to learn, was an honour for which many aspired, but few achieved. This was true education in ancient India. Similarly, in the Renaissance period apprenticeship of great masters was made possible to artists like Leonardo Da Vinci, and to others by gauging their innate ability. The fear of failing was overcome by the love to learn and to excel.

Vedic Prophecies talk of Karmic destruction that comes from unmindful actions of the society. These ravage the environment. Much exploited earth revolts, throws up lava, fires and more, waters get polluted by man's selfish activities, war, and outbreak of incurable diseases takes place. All this happens when man ignores his place in nature.

Education of nature held an important place in the student's life during Vedic times. The student considered himself to be a part of, and not a controller of nature. He was one of the many spokes of the wheel. To function was to move in harmony with nature and not to ravage it in the name of 'progress.' Trees were revered. Water was sacred. The same spirit breathes through us all.

We are embodied Spirit. Will we destroy our self?

Do we not see signs of viruses spreading because of man's failure to have reverence for life? Are we becoming asymptomatic carriers of evil viruses because we failed to be carriers of good habits, compassion, and kind consideration? Nature abhors a vacuum. We must be carrying something in our attitudes, minds, and hearts. What form of conveyor belts are we?

Compassion is the key to building peace and harmony with nature and avoid catastrophes like the pandemic. Buddha's middle path helps.

Some examples of signs are: **The Triad** is a sign of balance, harmony, wisdom, friendship, piety, and peace. Moses was guided by the signs. When Krishna was born, there was rain, thunder, and his imprisoned father was divinely commanded to take his child to his brother-in-law across the Yamuna.

Here Krishna grew up in a safe environment. Chains broke, prison doors flung open, as Krishna was carried by Vasudeva in a basket through the rising and falling waters of Yamuna to a haven. The story of Moses runs parallel to that of Krishna.

There are religious signs, cultural signs, commercial signs, medical signs, educational signs, road signs, signs of love, fear, guilt, shame and more. They are visible when we focus on them, we notice them, tread them. But do we comprehend them? We use them to investigate, to gather information, to feel the palpable, to brand, to interpret, to diagnose and to decipher. But can we relate to them by application in our lives? If so, how? This is the question we need to ask ourselves.

Signs of Buddhahood

"I can think, I can wait, and I can fast."
                                    – Siddhartha by Herman Hesse

Buddha was not a person. He was a state of mind. His name was Gautama Siddhartha. Buddha was the adjective derived from the Hindi word 'buddhi' meaning intelligence, insight, and wisdom. When he acquired these by following the middle path, he became a realized on or Buddha. The halo over his head is a sign of Buddhahood. He had several realized followers or bodhisattvas who followed in his footsteps.

This was a form of Buddhahood. Buddha was born after many prayers to the king of Nepal. At his birth which came after a long time, his father consulted a soothsayer as was the custom those days. Moreover, Buddha was born with a tooth in his mouth, so his father was worried. History tells us that the soothsayer predicted that Gautama Siddhartha as he was named at birth would leave the samsara in pursuit of self-realization. His father kept him surrounded by luxuries, married him to a nearby kingdom's princess. Buddha had a son. The sign still haunted his father. One day tired of his artificial life in the palace Buddha wanted to see the real world and stepped out of the gates of the luxurious palace.

Three signs that affected this renunciation and realization of the truth:

He first encountered an old man. He had never seen a man so bent, toothless and with sagged skin. He asked his friends: "Who is this?"

"This is old age," they replied.

Siddhartha asked, "Will I get old?"

"Sure, you will" they replied.

The next sight was that of a sick man.

"Who is this?" he questioned.

"This is a sick man" was the answer.

81

"Will I get sick?" he asked.

"Yes, anyone can get sick." they replied.

This bothered Siddhartha. He thought I must find a way out of this suffering.

The third sight was that of a corpse being carried by people for cremation.

"What is this?" he asked.

"This is death – the end of all." was the reply.

"Will I die?" he asked.

"Sure, you will" was their reply.

These were **the three signs** that made him realize the illusory nature of life and its gifts. They pass away. He realized the four noble truths: "Life is full of suffering, the cause of suffering is desire, suffering can be terminated by conquering desire. Desire can be conquered by following the eightfold path. Leaving his wife and son sleeping, he darned ordinary clothes and with a begging bowl in hand, left the palace for good, to seek 'His Truth.' (St. Francis of Assisi born of wealthy parents in Assisi had acted similarly).

People in the streets mocked Siddhartha; "Look at the prince with a begging bowl!" they said. Siddhartha's followers and friends were angered and wanted to fight the crowd. Siddhartha stopped them saying: "their **criticism is like a bowl of rice they offer.** I do not wish to take it. So, where is the need for anger? When you react, you accept anger, you accept the challenge of temporal power, the ego, the ignorance.

After much fasting, Siddhartha realized his body had become weak, but realization had not come to him. Austerity was not the way, but **balance** was. Excesses never got one anywhere, but moderation did. This was his moment of 'Awakening' – a sign of Buddhahood. He thus discovered the eightfold path to Nirvana. The story of Buddhahood is the story of self-realization in a temporal world. Love is its essence.

Among his other disciples was the great warrior, King Ashoka. The battle of Kalinga became a sign for king Ashoka that true victory lay over '**the hearts and not the lands of the people**.' His victory did not appease him. The sight of bloodshed began to sadden him, and he sought relief from it all in the teachings of Buddha. He sent emissaries to China, Japan, and Sri Lanka had edicts and pillars with Buddha's teachings erected far and wide. Gandhi ji followed the path of nonviolence in defeating the British empire and ousting them without weapons.

Will is 'crystallized intent' put into action.

I clearly remember the day of a great luncheon at the Savoy hotel in Mussoorie. I was eleven years old and overweight. This is not what I wanted to look and feel. So, I came upon a decision. If I could resist the grand spread this day, I would be serious in my intent to lose weight. It was this first step that was the most difficult. I put myself through this test. A difficult choice. Everyone around was feasting. The spread had umpteen dishes. All of these looked so appetizing.

History tells us that Buddhism was driven out of India by the monasteries becoming corrupt. The latter was a sign of its departure from India and adoption by other countries like China, Japan, and Southeast Asia.

Rigidity of the caste system became a sign for Gandhi to refer to the lower caste as 'Harijans' or children of God and ditag them. of its destruction. Labelling people like black, brown is always a sign of fracturing the universal humane in us. Inclusiveness is a sign of humility and equity. This writing is about becoming aware of the signposts as reminders on the journey, so we do not get beguiled by the superfluous, the unreal, the contrived, lies and manipulations. Being in the light facilitates moving ahead, staying on task, reducing worry, planning ahead and being in the moment.

Insights are signs that speak to us – messages we need to convey and converse with to make things happen. They are the voices from the voiceless speaking for liberation. Downtrodden by lack of appreciation communities and individuals descend into dark corners of their minds. When these voices find utterance through signs, they tell us of the impact statement of what happens when we ignore humanity in our march towards self aggrandisement. To be aware, conscious of our role in humanity, to reciprocate not react. Regrets are futile when we have the education, we need the foresight. Why do we shudder expression and at what cost?

The wisdom brought by insights helps us calibrate, inspires, and liberates and strangely we misinterpret it. The lens we wear si parochial to our conditioning and others' opinions. WE have a choice to stay in the rut or to evolve. A snail gets into the hole he burrows through. The Spirit flies high as it is not earth bound, but a guest on the planet earth.

How? If we have cared for it, listened, and reciprocated it will liberate us. If we have squashed it in preference to earthly gain, fame, we will have difficulty in releasing it from the body.

M.K. Gandhi, a Barrister in England, was different from 'Bapu,' the father figure to millions of Indians. His transformation from the barrister to the human being who felt for his people and fought for them took place by following a sign.

Gandhi experienced something that became a sign and a direction and a calling. While travelling first class in South Africa, with a legitimate ticket in his hand he was thrown out of the compartment by the ticket collector for being a colored man. The prejudice was that colored people should not travel first class, they could not afford it and even if they did it was inappropriate. In this game of what is appropriate and what is inappropriate Gandhi became a victim. But he chose not to be one. So, he used his humiliating experience to fight against prejudice, racism. His energy calibrated to a much higher level than that of the British empire. Hence, he got power over their force and could oust them with his policy of 'ahimsa' or non-violence. He had evolved. What brought about the transition? Did he see any signs? Yes, he did. How did this come about?

Colonialism and got India her freedom from British rule after a century. Gandhi hit a century by following the sign of Svaraj in every dimension of life to win over the British empire with the only weapon in his armoury – his will towards nonviolence and truth. He fought for what loyalty, not for individual names and places, but to vision and values. Similarly, when we stand up for truth, courtesy, transparency, and accountability we are honoring ourselves by honoring these values. They become our signature. It is misperception to think that our name is our signature. Our deeds of courtesy, kindness and reciprocation are. Silent is dumb before these Judgement does not measure but is a flaw to be measured. Its extent is carcinogenic to realizing potential. It stands on the threshold of transactions not transformation.

He was born with a tooth in his mouth This was a sign of events to come. His father consulted soothsayers to explain the mystery. It was foretold that Buddha

People wondered why at age eleven I was fasting. My parents and others in the room tried to convince me that I could begin my diet some other day. To my mind, the best way to begin was when surrounded by temptation. It had to be first victory over the self before it became victory over food. I went through the evening with a soda in hand observing and conversing.

My focus had shifted. Resolve does not come with age; it comes with intent. Will power and motivation follow. I did lose weight over two months. It was the first step to surrendering temptation. This helped me gain strength of purpose. It was a life lesson that saw me through many a difficult situation in life. A learning curve. In two months, I had reached my desired weight. Now, I could wear the dresses of my choice, my self-image went up. I felt a lot better by this victory over self. Victory over self builds confidence.

There were other signs that helped me to understand myself and the world around. Years later, on a quiet afternoon, when the entire class of at the Teachers' college at St. Mary's went to see the film, "Heidi," I stayed back to prepare for my psychology examination. This choice turned into a meeting with Klaus Brumbach.

It was my practice to pace up and down the beautiful corridors of the convent while studying. I remembered the slimming mantra: "When you can sit, stand, when you can stand, run." This kept excess weight off. While I was pacing up and down, I became conscious of someone in the vicinity. Looking up, I saw a man leaning against a van, standing by the corridor smoking a pipe looking at me. I became conscious of him. Blue eyes, hair the colour of burnt sienna. Who was he and what was he doing smoking a pipe in a convent, watching me pace up and down?

"Hello!" he said.

"Hello" I replied and got back to my pace.

"May I interrupt you; I'm interested in what are you studying so ardently?"

"Motivation," I said and returned to the chapter.

"Psychology?"

"Yes. I have a test tomorrow. You can quiz me when I am done." I wondered if he would do that, but he did.

"Sure," he said and waited.

He listened patiently to my answers. Often, he asked his own questions on the chapter and added to my knowledge. This was interesting.

I learnt that in many small ways we respect the culture of another, in ordinary ways. We can show inclusiveness and respect. "How did you know so much, are you a psychologist?"

I asked. He pulled out his business card and gave it to me. It read: 'Klaus Brumbach, Counsel General of Federal Republic of Germany.' Puzzled I looked at it twice and then at him. Unaware who I was talking to, made me blush.

I had spoken my mind, expressed my fears, just as I would to a friend, a classmate and here I was speaking to a counsel general.

"You the Counsel General of Germany?" I asked flabbergasted and "Hard to believe." Words fell out like hot bricks.

He smiled. "Does that make any difference? "I like your spontaneity,"

He made me aware and appreciated me. I saw the tiny laugh lines around his eyes and studied his face. He could very well be the Counsel General. The show was over. The bell rang. Time to go. Klaus smiled as I left and said he would be back the next day to finish the film and meet Sr. Elizabeth.

Why would he meet Sr. Elizabeth? I thought. *She was my teacher. Was he going to tell her about our meeting?* I really did not remember how candidly we had spoken, what all I had said and became anxious.

Rain pattered on the tin roof of the verandah. The scent of the earth pervaded the air blending with freshly cut grass and the scent of tobacco.

All eyes turned, as tobacco and convent did not go together. I turned my face and there was Klaus Brumbach – the Counsel General. The students were rushing to the auditorium once more. I stood and watched him come towards me.

"How did the examination go?' he asked.

"Good," I said, "and thank you for quizzing me."

"Want to celebrate?" he asked.

"Celebrate?" I inquired.

"Yes, I'd like to take you out for dinner. Frunze – the new restaurant in town – I believe it is good. Would you agree to come?"

I had never been asked for a date by a counsel general before. It was flattering. My prudent upbringing came in the way.

"I would not be allowed to. We have a strict schedule here." I mused.

"I have taken Sr. Elizabeth's permission," he said.

"And she gave it?" I was surprised.

"She was all praise and trusts you." was his reply.

"I'll be at the convent anyway. If you'd change your mind…" and he was gone.

Long after he left, trimmings of his words were still with me, as the van rolled out of the convent gates. My heartbeat increased. I was touched for the first time by an attraction and a conversation, and I wanted more of it. I could have had it. But something stood in the way. It was ignorance.

He did come the next day and waited at the same place. Only, I did not come down. I watched him from my window in the dormitory. Those were the most difficult moments – a part of me wanted to have another conversation with this intelligent person. Yet, conditioning kept me from reaching out. After a long wait, I saw the lights, heard the tyres screech, the engine start, and watched him depart. I could feel the crunch of the wheels, his thoughts, his disappointment as the rain poured that night and I heard it with a pounding and a pensive mind. I spent the next few days reminiscing.

The metaphor of the butterflies came to mind, Some, catch them, others watch them, yet others let them fly away. I had become conscious of being a woman in my own right. I had felt acknowledged. It felt different. He wrote to me from Bonn and sent pictures of the house he was building. Were I to come to Germany, he would host me? A smile came to my face. It was the last thing I would be allowed. Unseen Bars of fear held me back. We exchanged letters on the psychology of living and relationships, and I learnt about the culture and history of Germany from Klaus. After some time, we drifted apart, like the butterflies, carrying memories of flowers.

Decades later in 2017, I met another Counsel General of Germany at a cultural gathering at the India International Centre in New-Delhi. He gave me some information about Klaus Brumbach. He was alive, had travelled to Romania, and was heavily invested in culture. How soon time flies and becomes a memory, telling us who we were, and who we become in the war of love and fear.

Maître Upanishad

'Even as a man who is asleep awakes, but when he is asleep does not know that he is going to awake, so, a part of the subtle invisible Spirit comes as a messenger to the body, without the body being conscious of his arrival.'

Bibliography

The Book by Alan Watts, Publisher: Vintage Books New York, 1972

The Celestine Prophecy by James Redfield and Carol Adrienne, Publisher: Bantam Books London, 1995

The Celestine Vision by James Redfield, Publisher: Hachette Book Group New York, 1999

The Secret Language of Signs by Denise Linn, Ballantine Books, Random House 1996

God and the Evolving Universe by James Redfield, Michael Murphy and Sylvia Timbers, Publisher: Penguin Putnam Inc. New York, 2002

The Seven Mysteries of Life by Guy Murchie, Publisher: Houghton Mifflin Co., Boston Massacheusetts,1978

Mysteries of the Unknown – Powers of Healing – Editors of Time Life Books: Alexandria, Virginia, 1975

Only Love is Real by Brian L. Weiss, M.D. Warner Books Edition New-York, 1996

Everything Counts by Gary Ryan Blair – Publisher: John Wiley and Sons New Jersey, 2010

The Essential Mystics by Andrew Harvey, Publisher: Castle Books – Harper Collins New York, 1996

1,001 Symbols by Jack Tresidder, Chronicle Books, San Francisco, 2003

Mala Thapar is an Indo-Canadian poet, mystic, writer, educator, motivational speaker, teacher, and parent.

Cultural Awakenings is a book of insightful reading on human issues, that we all must face and educate ourselves. This clarifies assumptions and perceptions in dealing with others and ourselves. It is a mini manual of issues that matter to us daily. We must contend with these. Written in an experiential story telling manner, the writing hits home with examples. Questions make us probe into our inner selves. Recommended reading for all those who wish to go beyond the nitty gritty of superficial living, and apply learning to life, thus making life meaningful.

Cultural Conundrums is about seeing the world with different lenses so that 'different' is not 'alien.' The norms of the east and west sometimes bring about a clash of perceptions and create cultural conundrums. Much is lost in interpretation; much is misunderstood, and walls emerge where a bridge could easily connect. Hence, we need to revisit the norm, redefine the boundary of tradition and modernity and reinvent systems that speak the common language of humanity.

Signature Cultures is a series of poems that arise from the depths of personal experiences and personal living of life. Written by writer, teacher, artist and poet, Matahari V, these poems raise questions that have remained unanswered for ages. They offer a glimpse into the anguish and questioning of a soul that feels life crowding in and equally feels the need to be true to oneself.